CONEY ISLAND BEFORE THE NYPD

robert l. bryan

Published by robert l. bryan, 2023.

CONEY ISLAND BEFORE THE NYPD

First edition. July 26, 2023.

ISBN: 979-8223646365

Written by robert l. bryan.

For Meghan

INTRODUCTION

For as long as a great population has been crammed into New York City, residents have been looking for an escape, and the breezy beaches on the islands at the south end of Brooklyn quickly became a popular spot to do just that. The first developments on the shores of Coney Island were built back in the middle part of the 19th century, and ever since then, it has morphed into its own kind of quirky boardwalk with some really out-there amusements and attractions.

The first incubators for babies were attractions on Coney Island, because hospitals didn't believe that they would help premie babies survive any longer, and developers of Coney's amusement parks figured that they were weird enough to draw in some attention. It's definitely an escape befitting Brooklyn, home of most things offbeat, odd and interesting.

Back in its heyday, Coney Island was home to three amusement parks, called Steeplechase Park, Luna Park, and Dreamland. Eventually all were closed and replaced with a smaller park called Astroland. Astroland then closed, and another version of Luna Park opened up in 2013. The new Luna Park has tons of rides, and they currently operate the infamous Cyclone, a wooden coaster that's been thrilling riders since 1927, making it one of the oldest rollercoasters in America—it's even on the National Register of Historic Places!

Another famed Coney Island ride most are probably familiar with is the Wonder Wheel, also built in the 1920's and still kickin' today. If you dare to ride it, you can choose between a fixed car and a swinging car, which rocks and sways as the wheel turns. Throughout the island, you'll find other vintage rides, like carousels and bumper cars, mixed in with really modern coasters.

The hot dogs and historic rides aren't the only old-school attractions you can find on the island—you can also go see an authentic circus sideshow. From sword swallowers to fire-eaters and more, the

Coney Island Sideshow and Museum's rotating cast of characters will definitely fill the crowd with shock and awe.

At the Coney Island Sideshow's museum, you'll find one of one most notorious hoaxes in all of history: P.T. Barnum's Feejee Mermaid. In the early 19th century, Barnum began to advertise an exhibit featuring a "real-life" mermaid at his notorious American Museum. Barnum's museum mostly displayed freaks, exotic objects, and other bizarre attractions, and the mermaid (which was pretty obviously the top half of a monkey sewn onto the bottom half of a fish) fit right into his collection. Some hold that Barnum's mermaid was lost to one of the many fires that tore through his museum, while others claim it lives on at the Sideshow Museum.

Or, better yet, embrace the mermaid lifestyle for yourself. Coney's annual celebration of the start of the summer season is typically not-typical: it's a Mardi Gras-esque Mermaid Parade through the neighborhood. There's always a King and Queen, and lots of floats and crazy, elaborate costumes and contests during the event, which is always held the Saturday closest to the first day of summer. It's been a beloved tradition since the 1980's and has inspired other mermaid parades across the world.

Nathan's Famous Hot Dogs has almost become synonymous with "Coney Island". What started out as a Coney Island nickel hot dog stand run by a Polish immigrant in 1916 has quickly become one of the world's most-craved wieners. Al Capone, Eddie Cantor and Cary Grant all enjoyed Nathan's Famous Hot Dogs back in the day, but they really became famous when President Franklin Roosevelt served them to the King and Queen of England and had them shipped to Yalta during a meeting with Joseph Stalin and Winston Churchill. Nathan's is also famous for their annual July 4th Hot Dog Eating Contest—it's like the Super Bowl of Major League Eating.

Coney Island even has its own minor league baseball team. The Brooklyn Cyclones, whose stadium is just off the boardwalk, were named after the rollercoaster via a contest. They've been around since 2001, and are much beloved by their borough, which, despite their love of baseball, has been without a team since the Dodgers left for Los Angeles in the 1950s. In fact, the team's mascots, Sandy the Seagull and Pee Wee, are named for Brooklyn Dodgers players Sandy Koufax and Pee Wee Reese.

Whatever kind of offbeat adventure you're looking for, you'll find it on Coney Island. It's the perfect dreamlike summer escape from the hustle and bustle of the city.

Hot dogs, amusement parks, tourists, freaks... Coney Island is a pretty good representation of America, and a slice of what New York City is all about. Along with the crowds enjoying fun in the sun, however, will always be a small element of those intent on ruining the good times through criminal and anti-social behavior. Accordingly, a strong police presence is imperative to allow people to enjoy the events and attractions of Coney Island safely.

My first experience with policing Coney Island came as a rookie transit cop in 1982 assigned to the Tactical Patrol Force (TPF). TPF sounded impressive, but it was really the first stop for rookies out of the academy where the job was to ride subway trains between 8 PM and 4 AM. I was assigned to a TPF unit based in Queens, but one of my train runs was the F train, which runs through Queens, Manhattan and Brooklyn, terminating at Coney Island. During that summer on TPF I saw many interesting sights on those late-night trains pulling out of Stillwell Avenue. Besides the masses in various stages of intoxication, I recall several instances where people had live chickens with them on the train. There was also a man who had a rope tied around the neck of a pigeon and allowed the pigeon to fly around the car at the end of the rope. When confronted about the bird the man calmly stated it was his pet. In retrospect I suppose there would be no more appropriate New York City pet than a New York City pigeon. On several occasions I also had to deal with people who just didn't want their feasts to end. They had been barbecuing on the beach, but on the train, they were lighting charcoals to continue the barbecue on the train ride home.

In those days of the 1980s I represented just a tiny slice of the forces policing Coney Island. Before the Transit and Housing Police departments merged into the NYPD in 1995, Transit Police District 34 was located in the heart of Coney Island at Stillwell Avenue. Housing Police PSA 1 was also located in Coney Island. District 34 and PSA 1 still exist today, but they are Bureaus within the NYPD, whose 60 and 61 Precincts are the primary source of law enforcement for Coney Island.

The crowds, the fun, and the crime and disorder that unfortunately comes along with it are not a modern phenomenon. Long Before the NYPD was a presence on the island there was a need for law enforcement. Who were those law enforcers back in the 19th century? Let's take a look.

THE BEGINNING

On September 1, 1609, one day before he discovered Manhattan, Henry Hudson discovered Coney Island, a 5-mile-long waste of sand dunes, scrub grass and conies, the wild rabbits that gave the place its name. Despite its name, Coney Island was never an actual island, but rather separated from the rest of Brooklyn by a thin creek to its north. Its coastline is protected from harsh waves by a nearby barrier reef in the Atlantic Ocean which also served to change its size and shape between 1600 and 1800. Its shifting topography, crippling winter storms, and limited access from nearby Brooklyn and Manhattan hindered its early development.

While most of Long Island developed with the rest of urban New York City and the British Colonies, Coney Island would not flourish until after the Civil War. In fact, Coney Island was still a wasteland more than two centuries after Hudson's first visit when in 1847 a side-wheeler from Manhattan began tying up at a makeshift pier on the island's western end. Out on the beach men served clams and beer under a crude pavilion amidst raucous bouts of three card monte and games of dice called chuck-a-luck. It is a well-known fact, one visitor complained, that picnics are arranged for the sole purpose of pickpockets, prostitutes and swindlers.

Coney Island's orientation, stretching from east to west, provides for full sun all day along its five-mile coastline. This fortuitous geography led to Coney's only development prior to the Civil War - small resorts and restaurants along the coastline. It became a leisure destination enjoyed primarily by New York's elite. For them, Coney Island boasted seaside resorts, bathing attractions, and fine dining. Coney's seclusion and beauty offered these patrons both a psychological and physical separation from urban Manhattan and the restorative qualities of the ocean. As early resorts took shape in the 1860s to attract Manhattan's elite, Coney's more exclusive areas came to be known as Manhattan Beach at the far eastern end and Brighton

Beach further west. These beaches continued to be the destination of upper-class Americans, characterized as wealthy capitalists, manufacturers, merchants, and landowners. [1]

To cater to this affluent clientele, at the eastern end of the island, as far away as possible from the disorder of the west, three vast frame hotels went up. By the 1870s the Brighton Beach, the Manhattan Beach, and the Oriental Hotels were drawing respectable families and their servants for the whole summer. The proprietors piped in fresh water from the mainland, offered band concerts every evening. This is also where the first formal policing of Coney Island took place as hotel owners paid special police officers to patrol the beaches where the guests were mastering the difficult art of sea bathing.

Early developers created these retreats for America's "upper class" who sought temporary escape from Manhattan and northern parts of Brooklyn and had both the time and money to vacation. Pre-Civil War Coney Island still looked very much like it had when the first English settlers, led by Lady Deborah Moody, fled Puritan religious homogeneity in Massachusetts. The group settled Coney's neighboring town of Gravesend in 1643, just nine miles from Manhattan. The town of Gravesend, the original name for the Coney Island settlement, was the only colony in America founded by a woman. [2]

Following the Civil War, a period of dramatic change began to occur at Coney Island due to the rise of an urban industrial mass in Manhattan. Coney's proximity to Manhattan, a growing urban population, and improved transportation began to increase its popularity in the 1870s and 1880s. These changes enabled a corrupt element to seize the booming beach town and to install iniquitous attractions. As a result, saloons, brothels, prizefighting, horseracing, and gambling dens all found their place along the island, west of Coney's exclusive ocean resorts. These developing areas, known as West Brighton Beach and the Bowery, attracted a poor, uneducated, "working class" crowd from nearby Manhattan and Brooklyn. In 1880, many of this working class were among the estimated 2.4 million people employed by America's factory system, the center of which was Manhattan and Brooklyn. At Coney Island in the 1880s, New York City's working class began to find a reprieve from their urban conditions—poverty, crowding, and public neglect. As their leisure time increased investors saw an opportunity to profit from this working class and built more of what Coney's elite resorts did not offer—bars, brothels, dance halls, games, prizefighting, and gambling. This "rougher crowd" brought great profit to the aforementioned establishments. As a result, Coney Island's Bowery area became a bustling haven for commercialization, unrefined by Victorian standards. As the Bowery's popularity grew, Coney Island was criticized for harboring "vice," the contemporary term for immorality, crime, and corruption. Coney Island also became the focus of early "anti-vice" reform movements. [3]

People too poor for the east end of the island and too cautious for the west spilled out along a stretch of beach called West Brighton that was not yet built up by the big developers. By 1879 an Irish born builder named John Y. McKane had wrested control of Coney Island's political machine so completely that no building from a chowder stand to an iron pier went up without his approval. During McKane's reign the island became a showcase for the wonders of the machine age. In 1876 the centerpiece of the Philadelphia exposition was moved to Coney Island - an observation tower whose steam powered elevators lifted people three hundred feet above the sea. It was the tallest structure in the United States. Daring bathers could go for nighttime swims pulling themselves along ropes under the hissing blaze of primitive arc lights. People called it electric bathing. Afterward they could eat a novel kind of hot fast food. It's inventor, Charles Feltman, called them Coney Island Red Hots. Others, uncertain of their ingredients called them hot dogs.

Gravesend was the town immediately adjacent and to the north of Coney Island. After settlers acquired the land from native tribes, all of Coney Island was considered common land, owned by the town of Gravesend.

Few people realize that Southern Brooklyn has only been part of Brooklyn for little over a century. What is now Brooklyn, or Kings County, was originally divided into six self-governing towns founded in the 17th century on the southwestern tip of Long Island. Five of the towns were settled largely by Dutch immigrants; these came to be called Bushwick, Flatbush, Flatlands, New Utrecht, and Brooklyn. The sixth and southernmost town, Gravesend, was founded by a band of English religious dissenters who fled intolerant Massachusetts for the more hospitable climate of New Netherland (rechristened New York once the British took over in 1664). Eventually, the town of Brooklyn became an incorporated city, and between 1854 and 1896, absorbed each of its neighbors (Gravesend was annexed in 1894) until its borders equaled Kings County's. Brooklyn, in turn, became a borough of Greater New York City in 1898. Coney Island was considered to be part of the town of Gravesend.

The Bowery was located approximately two miles west of Coney's exclusive resorts, and slightly inland. The area was full of working-class patrons who, like the upper class, desperately sought to escape Manhattan and northern Brooklyn during the summer months. Like Coney's eastern end, the Bowery was developing quickly. New investments there aimed to profit from New York's working class, whose leisure time was increasing. Investors constructed better roads and rail lines to carry patrons. They built additional bathhouses and saloons that looked very different from Coney's exclusive resorts but were popular among working class patrons. As a result, this area was growing in popularity in the late 1870s, but its development was haphazard. The New York Times described the Bowery with the following:

The western end of Coney Island is naturally the finest section of that watering place, but it has always been disfigured by small houses, booths, and so- called hotels. The beach is obstructed by bathing-houses irregularly placed; there are no roads or paths, and a view of the sea is almost unattainable from behind the beach.

The disapproving tone of the article underscores the class divide that existed at Coney Island in these years. Unlike the expensive hotels at Coney's east end, the west end was known for its saloons, brothels, circuses, prizefighting, horseracing, and gambling dens. These businesses were not organized or capitalized like those of the eastern end, but they were affordable for the working class.

The creation of the Brooklyn Bridge in 1883 removed the last obstacle that kept masses on Manhattan. For working class patrons who could afford the train fare, Coney's beaches were a great retreat from the city. However, there was not much mingling between upper class and working-class visitors at Coney Island. They found their respective versions of leisure at opposite ends of the island throughout the 1870s and early 1880s.

Coney Island beach depicted in the late 1860s

Three Card Monte on Coney Island in 1870

The affluent east end of Coney Island

One of the large, luxury east end hotels

The upper class stroll the walk in front of a luxury hotel

A little girl poses for the camera on the affluent east end of Coney Island. A special policemen employed by the hotel keeps watch in the background.

A closer look at the special policeman

Crowded beach on the west end of Coney Island

Depiction of the view from the observation tower.

The observation tower

Nighttime bathing under electric lights – called electric bathing

Coney Island beach scene

The hotel (brothel) know as Elephantine Colossus

POLICING CONEY ISLAND

Until around 1835 the policemen of Brooklyn were the constables and deputy sheriffs along with some watchmen employed by private citizens and companies. As a matter of fact, there are records from 1785 reflecting just four policemen for all of Brooklyn - two constables and two watchmen. The work performed by these four law enforcers resulted in fifteen arrests and a total of $18 was paid to them. The arrests were mostly of farm hands who indulged in too much ale at husking parties and dances, and slaves who made unauthorized visits to chicken coops and melon patches. In 1834 the Village of Brooklyn became a full-fledged city, but there was no real provision made for a police force. The new municipal authorities of the city decided to keep the old system of law enforcement and simply told the population to hire their own private security if they felt the need.

As the city grew, so did crime, but there was great resistance to the establishment of a police force, especially from wealthy land-owners who feared a huge increase in taxes would be required to fund a police force. One of these rich anti-police crusaders is reported to have said in 1843, "I'd sooner be robbed and have my throat cut by thieves, and have the same thing done to my neighbors, than pay one cent for a damn policeman." The anti-police crusade, however, was a lost cause, and finally in 1850 the city of Brooklyn established a police department based upon the New York system. The first chief, or superintendent of the Brooklyn Police Department was John S. Folk. The autonomy of the Brooklyn police force did not last very long.

In 1857 the mayor of New York was Fernando Wood, destined to go down as one of the most corrupt politicians in the history of New York. He also forced each New York policeman to contribute to his campaign fund, but he was an ardent supporter of the police and their own financial corruption, creating a system where both he and the police profited. As Wood grew in power and the city government grew more corrupt, the state legislature took action. They created a new police force in the Spring of 1857, the Metropolitan Police, or "Mets," and abolished the Municipal Police, or Munis. The state effectively took direct control of policing in several districts, including New York and Brooklyn.

Members of the New York municipal force were reluctant to relinquish their jobs and continued to patrol the city's streets, often clashing with the metropolitan police over turf. While the courts attempted to resolve the problem, the two blue-coated forces competed with one another in arresting the ringleaders of the Bowery Boys and the Pug Uglies, gangs of hardened street toughs that terrorized New York. Eventually an agreement was reached, and many municipal officers joined the ranks of the Metropolitan Police.

Under the Metropolitan Police Act, the "Met's" were governed by three police commissioners and consisted of a general superintendent, two deputy superintendents, five surgeons, and assorted inspectors, captains, sergeants and patrolmen. All were outfitted in similar uniforms - the chief difference being the frock coat. Those worn by superior officers were double-breasted; all others were single breasted. In 1857, under Frederick Tallmadge, the first general superintendent, the Metropolitan Police District was divided into precincts, which in turn were subdivided into patrol beats. The precincts, some having more than one station house, were, each staffed with one inspector, one captain, four sergeants, patrolmen and officers assigned to details. In 1870, the State Legislature passed an act known as the "Tweed Charter" that returned police powers to the Municipal Police. Once again, Brooklyn had an autonomous police department. [4]

The responsibility for law enforcement at Coney Island was a bit confusing in its early days. Originally, all of Kings County was policed by the Sheriff's Office. Contributing to the confusion was the fact that in the records of the day, the terms "police" "deputy" and "constable" seemed to be used interchangeably.

Originally each of the city's five county-boroughs had its own sheriff, each of which held the widest law enforcement jurisdiction in their respective county-boroughs. Like most sheriffs in the United States, these office holders were elected to their positions. Once the city was consolidated in 1898, the New York City Police Department took over the responsibility of policing and criminal investigations throughout New York City, while the Sheriff's Office continued to focus on civil law enforcement and administering the county prison systems. Sheriffs were compensated by charging fees for enforcing civil orders in addition to keeping a monetary percentage (known as poundage) of what their office would seize. Sheriff Stillwell was the first Sheriff of Kings County in 1683, and James Mangano was the last in 1942, when the city's five county sheriff's offices were merged to become the Office of the Sheriff of the City of New York.

When Brooklyn became a city in 1834, several towns in Kings County remained independent. One of these towns was Gravesend which was unique among all the towns of Kings County because it embraced Brooklyn's maritime provinces of Coney Island, Sea Gate, Brighton Beach, Sheepshead Bay, and Manhattan Beach.

There was evidence of the Kings County Sheriff's Office providing law enforcement response in the independent towns of the county. For example, there was recorded police actions by Deputy Sheriff John Friend as far back as 1851 when he made arrests for rioting and stealing cows in New Utrecht. In 1858 Deputy Sheriff Friend arrested ten men for rioting in Gravesend when they roamed through the community destroying fences, and in 1878 Friend arrested a homeless man who broke into a reverend's Gravesend home and attacked him. [5]

The Brooklyn city force was responsible for policing Coney Island before the town police of Gravesend was established. Apparently, Brooklyn didn't place much importance on Coney Island because the only reference to a Brooklyn officer being assigned to the island was in a very sarcastic 1869 newspaper article. The story related how the police commissioners voted to detail one police officer to Coney Island for the summer of 1869 to take care of the three card monte men and rowdies who sometimes infested the popular resort. At the time, the Metropolitan Policing system was still in place and the article noted that out of three thousand men, the commissioners decided they could generously spare one. The article went on to hope that the selected policeman was big and that the commissioners would give him a velocipede (a type of early bicycle) to get over the sand rapidly.

I found reports of Gravesend police activity dating back to 1876. In one case a man got beyond his depth while bathing and was going down for the last time when officer Latham, of the Gravesend Police came on the scene, and waiting only to throw off his coat, rushed in and rescued him. The man gratefully offered him all he had - $3 as a reward, and on the officer's refusal to take it, was indignant to think that his life was not worth that. {6]

There was another report of an arrest made by Officer Baker. In this case, John Miller, twenty-five years of age, who was formerly a waiter at one of the island's hotels, was caught in the act of stealing from one of the bath houses of James S. Voorhees, by Officer Baker, of the Gravesend Police. He was taken before Justice Voorhees, who fully committed him for trial. [7]

In another case, Officer Butler of the Gravesend Police also saved a man from the effects of sun stroke. He had been deserted by his friends and would have died had he not been discovered by the officer, who had him taken to the hospital.[8]

There was also mention of a Gravesend Police force in a non-enforcement capacity in 1877 at the Methodist Union Picnic. It was noted in a newspaper article that the Gravesend police were well represented by John Whalen and James Williams who were specially detailed by Supt. Voorhies to keep all rowdies away. The reporter said he arrived late at the grounds, and could not glean many incidents, but he heard that Mr. John Bateman, 50-years of age beat Mrs. Voorhies in skipping the rope, and Unionville claimed the banner for the handsomest ladies.[9]

It was also noted that in 1877 the first jail was established in Coney Island. There had never been a tremendous need for a jail, but the feeling had been that one was required for times when it would be necessary to lock up unruly visitors who disturbed the general peace. The police would be more strict with infractions if they knew there was somewhere to secure a troublemaker. This problem was solved in 1877. Drunkards and rowdies could not only be locked up but also "cooled down" in one of Feltman's large ice houses, which were found to be perfect for use as a jail cell.

Charles Feltman began his career in 1867 pushing a pie wagon through the sand dunes of Coney Island. Four years later he leased a small plot of land and began building an empire that by the early 1900s covered a full city block and consisted of nine restaurants, a roller coaster, a carousel, a ballroom, an outdoor movie theater, a hotel, a beer garden, a bathhouse, a pavilion, a Tyrolean village, two enormous bars, and a maple garden. Feltmen is best remembered as the inventor of the hot dog.

The icehouse was a large structure and stood at the back of Feltman's pavilion. It has all the necessary strength and the padlocks on the door was such as might break the heart of the stoutest jail breaker. This icehouse had not been in use, as Feltman had to build a larger one for his consumption of ice had increased with his business. Police Justice Vorhees saw it and was satisfied, so Coney Island had a jail. The jail's first prisoner was a man named Andrew Walker, who was arrested by two Gravesend officers for an unknown charge and promptly put on ice. After he had been sufficiently cooled, he was taken before Justice Vorhees, who suspended sentence but warned him to be careful in the future. The icebox worked like a charm. [10]

It was also recorded that in 1876 John T. Hinman was elected constable in Gravesend and inspector of elections. There will be more to say about Hinman later.[11]

The story of policing in Coney Island is primarily the story of one man. At the center of the early boom years in Coney Island was a young Irish carpenter, John Y. McKane, born in 1841 and raised in Gravesend. When the Gunther Railroad first chugged into Coney Island in 1862, John Y. McKane was a 21-year-old living in Gravesend and learning the carpentry trade. By 1866, he had branched off on his own as a carpenter and builder in the Sheepshead Bay area. Two years later, in 1868, he got his first taste of public office when he was elected constable in Gravesend. McKane, while not handsome, had strong features set off by a broad-brimmed hat, mustache and carefully trimmed black beard. He had married a local girl, Fanny Nostrand, when he was 24 years old and settled down to raise three sons and a daughter. He didn't smoke or drink and taught Sunday school regularly at the Methodist Episcopal Church.

Diligent and hardworking, McKane continued to operate his construction business on the side. He also was appointed commissioner of common lands. Already, these positions were a blatant conflict of interest since McKane profited personally from the sale of public lands.

McKane was ambitious and a well-known businessman in the area. His contracting firm leased land to many of Coney's most popular proprietors, and he soon developed a reputation for dirty dealing. During Coney's early development, McKane personally profited from the sale of undervalued land. Crafting illegal leases and real estate deals became his specialty.[12]

In the course of obtaining building permits, McKane got to know the inner workings of the Gravesend town government. Decades earlier, in 1834, the State of New York had combined a number of towns (officially known as 'villages') at the west end of Long Island to form the City of Brooklyn. Five of these towns, including Gravesend, were allowed to retain their prior self-governing status. Their local governments had a great deal of autonomy as to what went on at the local level, including construction and the selective application of law enforcement.

Most of the farmers and businessmen of Gravesend and Coney Island viewed the day-to-day functioning of the local government as a bother and a bore. They were too preoccupied with their livelihoods to concern themselves with such tiresome intricacies. As long as those in charge saw to it that the peace was kept, that the garbage was collected, that the roads were repaired, that the taxes were within reason, and that the brothels were kept out of the public view, they were satisfied to let the job be done by others, particularly as the supervisory salaries were inconsequential.

McKane was not unmindful of such indifference towards political office and seized the opportunity. He realized that political influence would greatly benefit his construction business. It allowed him to obtain permits that others could not, rezone areas, hold up projects with red tape unless they used his company, and be in the thick of every major construction project.

In 1879 John McKane was elected Gravesend Town Supervisor over Supervisor Jaques J. Stillwell by a 39-vote majority, the total vote being 648. This was the highest position attainable in Gravesend, the equivalent of a city's mayor. As Town Supervisor, he had to keep a watchful eye on the Tax Department and Department of Licenses. Not to worry, for McKane was in charge of those departments as well. McKane magnanimously also served as Gravesend's Commissioner of Water and Gas and Commissioner of the Board of Health. [13]

By that time the beach at Coney Island was booming because it was so close to Manhattan by boat. When Boss Tweed became lord of Tammany Hall and brought in his corrupt friends to begin an era of lawlessness, they began spending their summer weekends at Coney Island. Pickpockets, confidence men, gamblers, strong-arm men and rowdies began to mingle with the upper class who frequented the beach. The resort area was within McKane's jurisdiction, but he found it prudent to look the other way. Despite its bad reputation, the big gamblers, politicians and their girlfriends continued to come, and in droves.

As Supervisor of Gravesend, McKane further consolidated power in 1881 by requesting that the city and state governmental authorities allow Gravesend to have its own police force. Gravesend had a quasi-independent governing body, but its police were provided by the City of Brooklyn and the Sheriff's Office and were hence a loose end in McKane's quest for power. He argued that Coney Island needed police who were specially trained in crowd control, and in the handling of the excessive number of troublemakers and drunks that congregated there.

Bolstering McKane's efforts to obtain his own police force was an incident that occurred during September of 1879. Some forty members of the notorious Cherry Street Dead Rabbits gang hired a ten-horse stage called the Pride of the Nation and embarked on a day of partying on the banks of Sheepshead Bay. Their commissary was well supplied with each "gentleman" carrying a bottle of whiskey and behind the Pride of the Nation meandered a wagon laden with kegs of lager. After meeting some tender maidens, the men partook in the festivities of the day which consisted of rioting and fights among themselves, drunkenness, rowdyism, profanity and obscenity of the most shocking character, nude bathing in full view of the hotels and railroad, robbing of the clam proprietors at the bay, theft and use of boats and other property, and finally an attempt to murder a clam owner who mildly protested their activities.

The Gravesend Police were powerless, for they were two against forty. At last, the day ended and the Cherry Street hoodlums, bearing with them the gentle maidens set out on the return voyage – the foulest, drunkest, noisiest gang of brutes that ever howled their way across the County of Kings, and made the streets of Brooklyn ring with their ribald shouts and songs. Meanwhile, the Gravesend Police had quietly taken a train to the city and notified the Brooklyn police of what had been done at Sheepshead Bay. An order was sent to Brooklyn Police Captain Woglom to capture the Pride of the Nation and all its passengers for the vile deeds done in Gravesend. The captain did this most effectually, surrounding the Pride of the Nation and its passengers at the ferry and causing the gang to march to the station house where the pedigrees of some 36 youths were taken. The youths were then placed in cells, and the next day transferred to the Raymond Street Jail, where they awaited examination by the Gravesend authorities. The young ladies were not held. These proceedings threw a pall over Cherry Street. That festive thoroughfare was ablaze with Chinese lanterns to greet its brave sons and fair daughters on their return from the shores of the far resounding sea. As one after another of the released damsels fled from the station house and flitted across the river to Cherry Street, they carried the news to desolate homes and disconsolate gin mills. Cherry Street doused its glim at once, hauled in its banners and emblazonry and rushed to Williamsburg; a mob of frantic women and children of indignant and riotous men who were ready to obliterate Captain Woglom, but the young roughs and their backers instead got a taste of Kings County justice from Brooklyn's Finest.[14]

The fact that it took an army of Brooklyn police to put a stop to the marauding gang served as ammunition for McKane's request for a police force. He increased his chance for success by offering to finance this force from the license fees and fines he collected, which could permit the City of Brooklyn to reduce its budget for the police department. As nothing pleases politicians more than to be able to show taxpayers that money was being saved, they granted McKane's request.

Governor Robinson signed the bill providing for an increase of the Gravesend police so that more patrolmen could be placed on the beach at Coney Island during the summer months. The bill granted $2000 a year which allowed for additional patrolmen during the 90-days of hot weather for protection of Coney Island. These officers served every year at a compensation of $2 a day. In 1878 the force consisted of 14 men and it was proposed to increase it in the summer of 1879 to 30.[15]

When word got out that there was to be a Coney Island police force, Kings County Sheriff Stegman was overrun with applications for appointments to the Coney Island force, but he had no business whatsoever with the police arrangements of that region. Supervisor John Y. McKane was in complete control of these appointments.[16]

John McKane had just one more detail to attend to. The Board of Police of Gravesend, of which McKane was president, held a meeting to make increased police appointments. The appointments to the Gravesend police force were made, but numerous special policemen appointments were also made, with these officers to serve without compensation from the town.

Most of the police presence at Coney Island was privately funded by hotels, racetracks, bath houses, and other places of business. These businesses hired, paid, and supervised their own officers, but all these policemen had to be sworn in as special policemen by the town of Gravesend. The Police Board had to approve each special policeman's application and the business had to pay the town a fee for each application.

Applications were not just rubber stamped. For example, at this meeting the board considered the appointment of James Lennon as special policeman at the Hotel Brighton, but McKane vehemently opposed the nomination saying the candidate was totally unfit for the position because of his drinking habits. The candidate was known as "Hungry Jim" and had already been on the police force and had been intoxicated and abusive while on duty.

The most important business of the meeting was the last item on the agenda. Town Supervisor John Y. McKane was appointed Chief of

Police. The new chief authorized the purchase of twenty policemen's badges to be furnished to officers at $3 each.[17]

With McKane running the police, word quickly spread that the fix was in. West Brighton, better known as Coney Island, became the roughest spot on Earth, and the change could be traced to when McKane got control of Coney's police force.

McKane's power in the town and on the island was absolute. He was often seen walking the beach with a giant club in his hand. He didn't need a salary as chief of police because the money to support the police force came from licenses issued by him. The fees ranged from $50 for guess-your-weight concessions to $250 for ring toss boards. And licenses for dance and music halls, bath houses, shooting galleries, saloons and carrousels were higher. Everyone paid tribute to McKane, and all learned to err on the side of generosity. McKane returned the generosity by issuing licenses to every low-life from every rat hole in New York who couldn't continue to operate an illegitimate business once the Tweed ring had been ousted. He granted them licenses to run saloons, gambling houses, carnival concessions and even fleabag hotels which were ripe for prostitution. They operated primarily along or near the Bowery and all were beholden to Boss McKane.

The position of police chief gave him a final say over Coney Island's vice and illegal activity. He donned a gold and diamond badge for the role. As chief of police he prevented any interference with his work, as town auditor he approved his own invoices, and as chairman pro tem of the Kings County Board of Supervisors he carefully paid those bills in full. As the town Supervisor of Gravesend, McKane was the head of every board and nominated all the remaining members. Simultaneously, McKane was the Town Supervisor, President of the Town Board, President of the Board of Health, President of the Water Board, Chairman of the Democratic and Republican parties, Chief of the Town of Gravesend Police Department, Chairman of Excise Commissioners, Chairman of the Highway Commissioners, Chairman of the License Commissioners, Chairman of the Commissioners of Public Lands, and Chairman of Sunday Schools, among other titles!

By 1884, McKane's construction company was credited with building nearly two-thirds of all buildings in Coney Island and Gravesend. Among these, he built nearly every hotel except for the three great hotels, the Brighton Beach, Manhattan Beach and Oriental. Apparently, the people who received great deals on the land McKane was renting to them understood that they had to kick back some of the money by hiring his construction company to erect their businesses. Given the frequent need to rebuild because of constant fires at Coney Island, there never was a shortage of work for McKane's company. McKane was successfully working other government angles while doling out deals as Commissioner of the Common Lands.

In 1884 the national election turned out to be exceptionally close, with the outcome hinging on New York State's electoral vote. Grover Cleveland and James Blaine were running neck and neck in New York State. The politicians in Democratic and Republican states and national headquarters were biting their nails as they watched the returns seesaw through the following day. Just when it appeared that there might be a tie vote in New York State, in came the returns from Gravesend. A jubilant roar almost lifted the roof of Tammany Hall. McKane had delivered the vote, several thousand for Cleveland, and barely enough for Blaine to compose a football team. Cleveland won New York by a little more than one-thousand votes. When McKane walked down Surf Avenue after the election, people gaped in awe at the man who had put Cleveland in the White House. McKane and a large delegation of his stalwarts were invited to Cleveland's inauguration. They paraded down Pennsylvania Avenue, and then attended the Inaugural Ball. When they got back to Coney Island, they were greeted like conquering heroes by a large crowd.

McKane was at the height of his power with all of Coney Island's political authority in his hands. He was corrupting the government from within, holding numerous positions simultaneously. As health commissioner, McKane could decide on a certain policy, as chairman of the town board he could order it implemented. Such a concentration of power meant that the small town of Gravesend had birthed its own version of what every large American city had: the urban machine "boss." John McKane threw his weight behind an even larger boss, New York City's Tammany Hall Democratic political machine. Tammany Hall's backing helped McKane eliminate local political threats.

As far as his police power was concerned, between the town officers and the special policemen employed by the larger hotels and other businesses, Chief McKane had under his control 150 police, 20 of whom are regular town police, the balance being the special privately funded officers. Police headquarters on Coney Island was originally located in a two-story frame structure east of Vandeveer's Hotel and the Plaza at West Brighton.

The methods by which McKane controlled Coney Island varied, but at the heart of his corruption was a certain tolerance for lawlessness and criminal behavior. His police force became known for its tolerance, proliferating some old "vices" at Coney Island, namely, gambling, prostitution, and prizefighting.

McKane became expert at determining how much of his corrupt activities would be tolerated by his constituency. When complaints against gambling and other vices would rise, McKane's police would take action, but only on a very limited basis. Police raids were conducted, but arrests were seldom made. This sham enforcement may have been enough to placate the citizenry, but the inaction did not go unnoticed by the press. The New York Times flatly asserted:

The hard-headed man of common sense who can waste no time on the sentimental relations existing between Coney Island gamblers and Coney Island policemen, and who advocates a vigorous enforcement of the laws, cannot fail to see that the excuses offered by those who ought to have enforced the law are puerile. He knows that there has been no attempt to prosecute those who have made parts of the island dangerous to honest men and have carried on their business under the eyes of complacent policemen. He regards the ridiculous raids as a farce, and he has a hearty contempt for officers who try to deceive taxpayers by sham at the eleventh hour.[18]

In Coney Island's Bowery, dozens of saloons and hotels were really fronts for profitable brothels that made the bulk of their money from prostitution. McKane was quite tolerant of brothels and prostitution on Coney Island reportedly saying, "houses of prostitution are a necessity on Coney Island." His comments were widely touted by the metropolitan press, further degrading Coney's reputation for the institutionalization of prostitution. Perhaps the best known of these brothels was The Elephant Hotel, completed in 1885. Called the "Elephantine Colossus" it was a fanciful, 150-foot elephant-shaped building, made from wood and tin, complete with guest rooms, stores, a dance hall.

To maintain supremacy, McKane had to exercise care in how he handled even the smallest of crimes. Theft was common in the Bowery, and it was a reoccurring topic of newspaper stories. That the newspapers covered so many stories of theft at Coney Island was perhaps unfair, since pickpocketing was common throughout New York City. Thieves often made the headlines and their stories further wrecked Coney's reputation among readers.

For example, a gentleman went to the Coney Island police station and reported his gold watch had been stolen. Chief McKane dispatched Detective Sullivan to investigate the theft. Sullivan returned to the station in less than thirty minutes in possession of the stolen watch. McKane was thrilled with the detective's quick work and asked if he would be able to find the thief.

Sullivan said, "Of course I could, but why would I want to do that?"

"To arrest him for stealing the watch," McKane bellowed.

"I can't do that," Sullivan explained. "I told him I would grant him immunity if he gave the watch back."

McKane was outraged as he addressed the detective. "If you do not go out immediately and arrest the man who stole the watch, I will lock you up for being an accomplice to the crime."

Sullivan chuckled at the threat, but five minutes later, with the assistance of two other officers inside the station, Detective Sullivan found himself locked in the cell.[19]

Clearly, McKane's determination was more the product of convenience, not of genuine concern for the law he was charged to uphold. Other illegal activities thrived at Coney Island under John McKane. For example, he sanctioned prizefighting, a controversial pastime that combined bloody, knock-out boxing matches with gambling. Betting on these purse fights was illegal in the State of New York, which was perhaps why the attraction was exclusive to Coney Island. The fights attracted thousands of onlookers to McKane's own Coney Island Athletic Club and were a great source of personal profit for him. Under McKane's rule, Coney Island became the "prizefighting mecca" which projected Coney's image as a place apart to a national audience. The prizefights were highly lucrative for McKane and the sponsors.

Prominent Coney Island businessman George Tilyou knew that sanctioned prizefighting was damaging Coney's reputation irreparably. His concern was real for his own resorts were losing high-brow customers. When he advocated for an end to the purse fights, he was in direct confrontation with McKane. As a result, McKane revoked Tilyou's lease.

McKane often succeeded in quieting his discontents, but the episode does suggest that tensions were mounting against him. Newspaper coverage of vice and McKane's corrupt hold on Coney Island led to increased criticism from churches and moral-minded citizens. When asked about vice at Coney Island, McKane once retorted: "There is no place in the world where there was less crime in proportion to its transient population than there is in Coney Island. Why gentlemen, we succeeded in keeping this resort free from gamblers and hoodlums last season, and we'll do it again this year."

To run his machine meant McKane often had to put on a show. To extinguish growing anti-vice sentiment, McKane orchestrated dramatic raids on gambling dens and saloons in the Bowery. He was constantly reaffirming his commitment to a vice-free Coney Island: "It is a pleasure ground and I mean it to be a harmless one," he said to The Times, "The ocean's coming up and we'll all be swamped soon, but we'll go down pure, or know the reason why." In his shrewdness, McKane knew it was easier to make a show of rectitude, occasionally giving in to public opinion. Within this context, the Bowery was an intense epicenter of vice. A growing immigrant and working-class population was fueling the demand for low-brow recreation there. Coney Island in these years was characterized as a "world unto itself," "Sodom by the Sea," and an "uninterrupted French fete." These characterizations captured Coney's vice well, but they understated McKane's contribution there. The primary accounts of what occurred under his rule demonstrated that McKane himself was very much responsible for shaping Coney Island in those years. He controlled the chaos only as much as was advantageous to him. John McKane had things his own way in Gravesend and on Coney Island, but that was about to change.[20]

John Y. McKane

In one of the ice houses of Feltman's Pavilion was located the first Coney Island jail.

Sheepshead Bay in 1876

The west end of Coney Island

The Coney Island Jockey Club

INVESTIGATIONS

"Houses of prostitution are a necessity on Coney Island, and I don't propose to interfere with the gambling at Brighton Beach and Sheepshead Bay. Afterall, this ain't no Sunday school."

– John Y. McKane, Chief of Police

With all the power he gained, John McKane also gained many enemies in the press, politics, and anti-corruption and vice organizations. Investigations regarding his failure to enforce gambling and other laws in Coney Island began occurring with a degree of frequency. Some of these investigations provide an insight into McKane's police department and his feeling of invincibility. A good example is some of McKane's testimony from a New York State Assembly Committee investigating illegal gambling at Coney Island.

McKane's testimony

Q. - How long have you been supervisor of Gravesend?

A. - I was elected in 1879.

Q. - Where do you reside?

A. – I have resided in Gravesend for 42 years.

Q. - When was it that Coney Island first came into prominence as a place of resort?

A. - 1880 or 1882

Q. - What are the departments – executive, judicial and financial in Gravesend?

A. - Supervisor, four justices of the peace, town clerk, commissioner of highways, and constable.

Q. - Are there not certain officers known as trustees?

A. -Yes, trustees of common lands.

Q. - Where in the village is police headquarters?

A. - 8th Street near Surf Avenue.

Q. - How far is police headquarters from Culver's railroad depot?

A. - In a direct line 1000 feet to the northwest.

Q. – What is the John Y. McKane Association?

A. - The John Y. McKane Association is a Democratic association with more than 250 members.

Q. – And what is the John T. Hinman Association?

A. – It is also a Democratic association with more than 300 members.

Q. – Who is John T. Hinman?

A. – John T. Hinman is a captain of police for three months a year appointed by the Board of Police.

Q. – Who is president of the Board of Police?

A. – I am.

Q. – As Town Supervisor, what other positions do you fill?

A. - President of the Board of Health, president of Town Board, president of Police Board, president of the Water Board, and the Board of Town Auditors.

Q. – Are you president of all these boards?

A. – Yes.

Q. – What is the composition of the Board of Police.

A. – Four justices of the Peace and myself.

Q. – And the composition of the Police Department?

A. - In 1883 there were 17 policemen appointed for 120 days a year – from June 1 to October 1.

Q. – What about during the winter?

A. - During winter there was no police – no money.

Q. – Has the police force increased since 1883?

A. - By 1887 police increased to 22.

Q. – What about special officers?

A. – There are 75 to 100 special officers – appointed to Culver's Railroad, Sea Beach Railroad, Gunther's Railroad, Iron Pier, and other places, like the hotels and racetracks. These places applied for a special officer and the Police Board appointed them.

Q. – Aren't the policemen employed at the Sheepshead Bay track employed by Mr. Pinkerton?

A. – Yes, they are.

Q. – Did the Police Board swear in these Pinkerton men as special policemen?

A. – We did.

Q. – Did the Police Board have the qualifications of these men to decide on their appointments?

A. – No, we relied on Pinkerton to provide only qualified men.[21]

Another investigation was conducted by State Senators Browning and Holmes regarding leases of land on Coney Island, where in some instances the leases were obtained fraudulently and in other instances at ridiculously low prices. The investigation was commenced by this senate resolution:

Whereas it is alleged that the present trustees and former commissioners of the common lands of the town of Gravesend of the County of Kings have, through a system of employing "dummies" representing themselves, acquired the title by leasing and otherwise of said lands, and also receiving fraudulent proposals for the sale of lands without properly advertising the same, have thereby defrauded the people of the town of Gravesend of large sums of money which would have been received had the trustees of said town honestly discharged their duties.

Once again McKane was called to testify.

Q. - What is your name?

A. - John Y. McKane

Q. - Where do you live?

A. - Sheepshead Bay

Q. - Do you hold any office?

A. - That of supervisor

Q. - What are your duties as Supervisor?

A. - To attend the meetings of the county board and pay the bills that are audited by the board and generally to attend to that part of the business of the town not governed by special laws. I was one of the commissioners of common lands prior to 1883. After that they were called trustees.

Q. - And you, as one of that board had the leasing of these lands?

A. - I was one of three. I hold some mortgages on Coney Island.

Q. - Where do you hold these mortgages?

McKane displayed his contempt and lack of concern for these investigations with the tenor of his response.

A. – I hold that it is not a fair question to ask me. I think it is impertinent. I can hold a mortgage wherever I please. That is my own private business. I will answer any fair questions about other matters, but I don't mean to begin to tell you my private business.

Q. – I submit it is fair to ask you who were the leases in these instances.

A. – I tell you I do not intend to answer, because I think the question is impertinent.

Q. – Do you decline to answer because the answer would jeopardize your interests?

A. – No; but because I think the question is impertinent. I can hold mortgages where I please.[22]

There was no question that illegal gambling was rampant at Coney Island. Section 351 of the penal code of the State of New York made gambling a crime. Section 117 stated that a public officer who willfully neglected his duty was guilty of a crime. John McKane was seen in full view of gambling that was against the law, specifically pool selling, a form of betting on races popular during the 19th century. McKane claimed that the racetracks afforded employment to many Gravesend people and brought money into the town.[23]

McKane's claim of money coming into the town could not be disputed. Almost 5,000 people were on the Brighton Beach Racetrack one summer afternoon. A pretty close calculation showed that there was about $80,000 invested in auction and French mutual pools in the five races that were run off. The pool seller commission being 5%, he realized the handsome sum of $4,000 from the investments of the outsiders. Mr. Engerman, the only proprietor of the track, ran the pools, the bars, the lunch stands and program business himself. He gave about $1,200 in purses each race day, which was more than covered by the paid admissions to his track. His expenses, outside of the purses, were about $700 each race day, which were nearly met by the profits of his bars, lunch stands, and sales of programs. Programs sold for ten cents each and were printed for Mr. Engerman for $5 per thousand. No wonder Mr. Engerman refused the offer of $150,000 by the Coney Island Jockey Club for his track.

Every few feet on this track one met a uniformed man with the shield of the Gravesend Police on his breast. There didn't seem to be the need for half of these uniformed men as the crowd was good natured and orderly. A reporter got hold of McKane to ask him some obvious questions about the activities at the racetracks.

Q. - What are you going to do about gambling on the island?

A. - I am going to stop it.

Q. - You mean gambling with cards?

A. - Yes, I won't have one of those places on the island if I can help it.

Q. - What about pool rooms. Will you have them?

A. - I don't want any of them

Q. - Will you close them up?

A. - I have already given notice to several parties who were about to open new places that they must not.

Q. - What about those who have already opened and are in operation?

A. - Next Sunday we shall have an increased police force and then I shall see what I shall do.

Q. - You don't favor their existence?

A. - I do not. I think they are demoralizing. They attract boys and needy men.

Q. - You have the power to suppress them?

A. - I believe I do.

Q. - You also have the power to suppress pool selling on the track?

A. – Yes.

Q. - Shall you?

A. - I don't think I shall. I have heard no complaints against it from the people of Gravesend and I believe I am carrying out their wishes when I leave it alone. These tracks afford employment to a great many Gravesend people and bring a good deal of money into the town. Of course, I am prepared to do whatever the people of this town desire me to do, but I have heard no complaints from anyone about pool selling on the tracks.[24]

The Kings County District Attorney also set his sights on McKane. District Attorney Catlin said there was no question that gambling had been carried on at Coney Island. He said he had no conception of the extent of the practice until recent developments. As soon as he received trustworthy information on the subject, he communicated with Police Chief John Y. McKane, of Gravesend. He said McKane expressed astonishment at the existence of the gambling places called to his attention and said that he was gratified at Catlin giving him the information.[25]

McKane always tried to give the impression that he was being responsive to complaints of criminal activity, so it was normal for the chief of police to say that as soon as the season opened at Coney Island he would endeavor to stop gambling and other games which were in progress. District Attorney Catlin followed up with a formal interview of McKane, in which McKane continued to be bold enough to express his intent to not fully enforce the law.

Q. - When will you organize the police force?

A. - About July 1st, and then all the gambling houses on the island I have knowledge of I will raid.

Q. - When you make the arrests what will be the results?

A. - I will leave that to the magistrate. All I can do is make the arrests.

Q. - The season opens on May 30th, that leaves over a month before the police are engaged. What will you do in that time?"

A. - Well, the town receipts do not warrant any exposure at present, and we have figured from July 1st, but, nevertheless, I will have special men employed from May 30th.

Q. - What kind of houses do you intend to raid?

A. - All houses in which faro or other games are played and also all places where pools are sold.

Q. - Do you intend to include the racetracks?

A. - No, as far as the racetracks are concerned, I see no reason why they should be interfered with. The tracks furnish employment of a legitimate character to many men who are residents of Gravesend and other country towns.

Q. - Why do you not intend to raid the tracks?

A. - Well, I don't mean to uphold gambling, but it is like liquor selling and liquor drinking. It only becomes a vice when use to excess.[26]

John McKane's arrogance in overlooking some of the gambling laws may have been in part the result of the tacit approval provided by some important politicians, including the Mayor of Brooklyn. Mayor Seth Low may not have been aware that he was being quoted by defenders of gambling at Coney Island, like John McKane, as favoring the systematic disregard of the law against pool selling. His vote in the Board of Supervisors may not have given that interpretation though it certainly indicated that the mayor was not opposed to the legalizing of pool selling on racetracks. The mayor voted no on a resolution introduced by Mr. Barnes embodying a protest by the supervisors against the pool bill, and a request that the members of the legislature from Kings County should use their best efforts to defeat it. The mayor accompanied his vote with the somewhat ambiguous remark that if he were a member of the legislature he would know how to vote on the bill, but as a member of the Board of Supervisors and a representative of the city he did not know. The mayor evidently did not think it worthwhile to make it perfectly clear as to which side of the question he stood on. John McKane, the managers of the racetracks and the leases of the pool selling privileges had no difficulty in placing the mayor. His name, which stood as a synonym for pure administration and reformed politics was held to be subscribed not only to the opinion that the prohibition against pool selling should be repealed, but that while it remained on the statute book it may, with entire propriety, be disregarded.[27]

Just about all of Gravesend's police operations were entwined with politics. As previously mentioned, the Gravesend Board of Police had to approve the applications for special policemen submitted by the hotels, racetracks and other businesses on Coney Island. Approval of a special policeman application was usually a simple process. If the applicant paid the application fee the special policeman was usually approved. That is, unless the applicant had the audacity to cross John McKane. Such was the case for a man named Devlin.

One afternoon a man bathing at Mrs. Vanderveer's bathing pavilion slipped under the water and had to be pulled unconscious from the surf. The tall stout man was taken to Mrs. Vanderveer's pavilion where Dr. Walker, of the Sea Side Sanitarium unsuccessfully tried to resuscitate him.

Mr. Devlin, a police justice took charge of the body in the absence of the coroner. There was a fee of $8.25 due to the justice if the coroner did not appear within 12-hours. Justice Waring, also a police justice, heard about the death and hurried to Mrs. Vanderveer's pavilion to claim the $8.25.

Under a decision of the Court of Appeals, the election of Devlin and Waring was declared illegal. In a subsequent election Waring was elected but Devlin was not. Since then, the feelings between the two had been very bitter.

When Waring arrived on the scene and claimed the right to the body Devlin tried to throw him out. A fight between the two ensued, causing disgusted onlookers to claim they were acting like vultures over the body. Devlin won the fight, but Waring ultimately had Devlin arrested for assault. Justice Williams, who took Devlin's place as a justice, demanded $200 bail.[28]

Mrs. Vanderveer, the owner of the bathing pavilion where the man had drowned, wanted to hire a special policeman to protect her business, but was refused when she applied to Chief John McKane. Mrs. Vanderveer complained to a reporter from the Brooklyn Union who confronted Justice Stryker, a member of the Gravesend Board of Police. When asked why Mrs. Vanderveer's request was denied Stryker had the following exchange with the reporter.

Q. – Why wasn't her request approved?

A. - She did not make the request in the proper manner.

Q. - How did she ask for it?

A. - She has not applied to the Gravesend Board of Police. I am the Secretary of the Board, and I ought to know.

Q. - But she applied to the Chief?

A. - That may be, but I don't know anything about it.

Q. - You mean to say that she ought to make a written application to the board?

A. - Yes, I will give no consideration to any request not made in writing.

Q. - Mrs. Vanderveer says positively that she sent a man over to the chief with a request. How does that meet with your view for a request?

A. - That's just where the whole matter hitches. The man she sent is not a fit person to be appointed.

Q. - But he was an officer last year?

A. - Yes, and during the fall elections he worked against some of the police justices.

Q. - And those men who are on the board refuse to appoint him?

A. - That's it.

Q. - But that is allowing politics to enter as a consideration in the matter of appointment, is it not?

A. - Yes, and that man will never be appointed by the board. Let Mrs. Vanderveer recommend someone else, and he'll get the appointment.

Q. - What difference does it make to the board – she has to pay the officers?

A. - Yes, but we appoint, and she is trying to force us to appoint him; but we won't and that's all. She is trying to play a game she cannot carry out. We do not refuse her police protection, but she can't get that man appointed.

Q. - But that is allowing politics to interfere with the duties of the board, and I scarcely believe they would do that.

A.- Oh, yes, they will in his case.

Justices Waring and Williams accused Devlin of working against them during the previous election and their feud had been bitter, so when Mrs. Vanderveer applied to the police board (which consisted of the police justices and McKane) to have Devlin hired as a special officer at her pavilion, they refused and stated publicly that Devlin would never be appointed.[29]

The accumulating investigations did not top McKane from modernizing his police department. In 1885 work began on a police headquarters that included a courtroom, cells, and offices. The construction was estimated to cost about $2,000. The second floor would be occupied as a court room, while the first would be divided into cells. John McKane would now have a comfortable place to try his cases, and it would also eliminate the necessity of conveying all prisoners to be tried at Gravesend Town Hall.[30]

In 1873, Anthony Comstock created the New York Society for the Suppression of Vice, an institution dedicated to moral supervision of the American public. Comstock successfully influenced the United States Congress to pass the Comstock Law, which made illegal the delivery by U.S. mail, or by other modes of transportation, of "obscene, lewd, or lascivious" material, as well as prohibiting any methods of production or publication of information pertaining to the procurement of abortion, the prevention of conception and the prevention of venereal disease.

Some of Comstock's ideas of what were "obscene, lewd, or lascivious" could be seen by many modern westerners as ludicrous, but during his time of greatest power, some anatomy textbooks were prohibited from being sent to medical students by the United States Postal Service.

In 1885 Mr. Comstock became the sharpest thorn in John McKane's side. In speaking of the Brooklyn Police Department Comstock said that years of experience had shown that in that department there were men who could not be corrupted by gamblers gold nor hoodwinked into allowing crimes to exist in violation of their oath of office, even if called upon to do so by would be respectable politicians. He asked why then should there be a crime ridden section of Kings County whose police force was precisely the reverse of Brooklyn's police. Why should the peace officers of Coney Island be passive daily spectators to breaches of the law which they had sworn to enforce. Comstock concluded that maybe it was because John McKane sat passively in his little police headquarters while laws were disregarded all around him.[31]

McKane knew that forces were closing in around him, so he always tried to hold these investigative bodies at bay by putting on big shows of selective law enforcement. He made herculean efforts to obtain credit for doing his duty as Chief of Police of the town of Gravesend, by causing raids to be made among a few of the small resorts of a vile character in the disreputable portion of Coney Island known as "the gut." The result was usually a few women being captured and arraigned and then adjudged as vagrants.[32]

McKane also endured a personal tragedy in 1885 when John McKane, his eldest son, died at his father's home in Sheepshead Bay, of pneumonia. The 18-year- old was in the hardware business, and the fatal attack was his second, as he had just recovered from the first one.[33]

It wasn't long before Anthony Comstock was back in John McKane's life. The Police Chief was sitting in his office at Police Headquarters when four of Comstock's men entered and informed him that they wanted to see him on very important business. They informed McKane that they were sent to Coney Island to get evidence against the pool sellers at the Brighton Beach Race Track and needed a couple of McKane's police officers to accompany them.

McKane was still unable to mask his arrogance and told the men that if there was any information to be obtained on Coney Island, he would be the one to get it, and that he would not have outside parties coming down attempting to run the island. McKane immediately summoned a coach and proceeded alone to the racetrack where he promptly arrested Mr. A.H. Battersby, secretary of the Brighton Beach Racetrack. McKane told a reporter he was not about to allow Comstock to run Coney Island and would not give his men the privilege of making the arrest.[34]

The press was becoming increasingly hostile toward McKane. This 1886 article in the Brooklyn Union was typical of the sentiment toward McKane.

Who is responsible for the disorderly character of West Brighton? Why is it that respectable people can visit one end of the island without any fear of having their sense of propriety shocked but cannot safely visit the other? The managers of Brighton Beach and Manhattan Beach employ their own police and take supervision of the property in which they are interested.

West Brighton is under the control of John Y. McKane and his associates of the Town of Gravesend. It is policed by a force over which McKane takes personal charge. It is, therefore, the fault of McKane that it is crowded with low resorts, and that law and order are openly defied within its borders. If either the chief of the force or its members understood their duties and performed them properly the west end of the island would not be so favorite a resort of black-legs, confidence men and dissolute characters as it is. McKane has for four years managed the police of the town of which he is "boss", and during that time West Brighton has gone from bad to worse until it is now deserted by all persons who have any regard for their character. It must be manifest that no improvement can be expected while McKane continues to fill the office. How is change to be brought about? General Jourdan believes, and his belief will be generally shared, that Coney Island ought to be governed by Brooklyn. He thinks that such police protection as the city enjoys would prove very advantageous to all the county towns.[35]

Meanwhile, Comstock had widened his web to include the Kings County District Attorney, now James Ridgeway, who he accused of standing by and doing nothing while law enforcement was ignored in Coney Island.

The accusations against Ridgeway were accompanied by a letter from Mr. Comstock, to Governor David Hill.

September 8th, 1886

To His Excellency, David R. Hill, Governor of the State of New York, Albany, N.Y.:

Sir- I have the honor to call your attention to the fact that in December, 1884 there were certain charges pending before Your Excellency concerning the non-enforcement of the law by James W. Ridgeway, District Attorney of the County of Kings against gambling by a committee consisting at that time of Messrs. H.E. Simmons, William C. Beecher, and myself, who waited upon you, and that these charges were, at your suggestion, withdrawn. At that time, it was suggested that the papers should be put in due form, and the charges all united and verified before Your Excellency took action.

After we had thus received the papers from Your Excellency, one of our committee was waited on by Mr. James R. Ridgeway, who in writing, in most positive terms pledged himself to do all in his power to secure the proper enforcement of the law in Kings County. That promise Ridgeway has broken in every particular, so far as my knowledge goes; and I am confident that it was simply a trick upon his part to secure delay, and to prevent us from returning the charges which we had made against him to Your Excellency for action.

The Brighton Beach Racing Association at Brighton Beach in the town of Gravesend, has since 1883 openly violated the laws of this state. In September 1883 we secured the indictment by grand jury of a number of those gamblers, and also the indictment of John Y. McKane, Chief of Police of the town of Gravesend, and several of his subordinates for being present, aiding and abetting these crimes and allowing them to go on without informing against or prosecuting them.

In May of 1881 Mr. Rideway wrote to McKane calling on him to enforce the law. He issued several proclomations through interviews with the daily press, in which he admitted that the violation of the law was open and flagrant, and that it was his intent to enforce the law.[36]

District Attorney Ridgeway immediately attempted to pass the buck. He pointed out that Brooklyn Chief of Police Patrick Campbell, a staunch advocate for eliminating pool selling and all forms of illegal gambling, had the power to break up pool selling anywhere in the county, including Coney Island, and that Campbell admitted he possessed this power. But when Ridgeway urged the chief to take action in Coney Island, Campbell replied that to do so would be discourteous to Chief John Y. McKane.[37]

While the investigations and indictments of John McKane seemed to go nowhere, McKane and his cronies settled comfortably into their offices in the new police headquarters at Coney Island located on the new 8th Street, recently laid out from the creek to the ocean. The building was about four times the size of the old edifice, and besides a courtroom, it contained five offices and as many cells.[38]

A new firehouse went up alongside it. The unofficial headquarters of Police Chief McKane was Ben Cohen's Albemarle Hotel on Surf Avenue where McKane liked to sit on a veranda of the and keep an eye on the crowd moving along Surf Avenue.

With all the scrutiny his police department was receiving, McKane was smart enough to realize that his periodic shows of enforcement were required, even if the enforcement was an ongoing farce that the public had grown accustomed to. For example, in one instance arrests were made by Under-sheriff Hodgkinson and five deputy sheriffs. A Union reporter was sent down to Coney Island to report on a raid that Chief McKane had announced would take place. Upon arriving the reporter saw Hodgkinson, two of his deputies, and one of McKane's pet officers known as the "woman hater" standing on Paul Bauer's stoop facing Paul Bauer's Club House. It was evident that no raid on the pool sellers was intended. They merely arrested certain employees at Bauer's pool selling establishment who had interfered with Deputy Sheriff Middleton in the discharge of his duties the week before. Just prior to the arrest of these men one of the proprietors of Paul Bauer's club house was in McKane's office, and immediately after the arrests they went to Paul Bauer's hotel and sat down for dinner together. The arrests were made in a very quiet manner and the pool sellers were not disturbed in the least.[39]

Another committee was formed to investigate the serious allegations levied against McKane and his department. The report of the 1887 Bacon Investigating Committee's investigation of illegal gambling on Coney Island indicated that, "It is well known...that the sheriff's officers have already been assaulted by the local Gravesend police" and that "every official in the County of Kings is aware of the fact that illegal gambling was taking place in the open, and especially the police of Gravesend." Still, John McKane continued with business as usual.

John McKane could not run the day-to-day operations of the police department by himself. He appointed one of his closest confidants, John T. Hinman, captain of police. As a testament to their friendship, one had to look no further than the two largest Democratic political clubs in Gravesend - the John Y. McKane Association and the John T. Hinman Association.

Captain Hinman shared McKane's philosophy for enforcing the laws of Coney Island very selectively. For example, in the rear of a well-known hotel on Surf Avenue it was not uncommon to find sports from Philadelphia and Brooklyn witnessing cock fights. The room was always densely crowded, and no attempts were made to keep the affair quiet or secret. This lack of concern of discovery was probably because one of the regular spectators was John T. Hinman, the Captain of the Coney Island Police. This gentleman took such an interest in the battles he would not allow the chickens to be placed in the pit until he saw their gaffs were properly adjusted, and he made no effort to conceal his identity.

During one short and decisive battle one of the Philadelphians shouted with joy as he saw the bird he was backing make the feathers fly. Captain Hinman grabbed him by the coat, pushed him against the wall and told him that if he did not keep quiet he would throw him out of the room. It looked for a time as if there would be trouble, as the Philadelphian showed fight. Quietness, however, was restored, and the battle went on. The bird backed by the sports from the city of brotherly love was defeated and they all left the island broke.[40]

Captain Hinman paraded around Coney Island wearing a handsome gold shield bearing his name as captain on its front with the words "presented by his friends" on the reverse side. The captain, who was the first policeman ever appointed to serve in the town of

Gravesend had the badge presented to him by Assemblyman C.J. Kurth.[41]

John McKane did not seem particularly bothered as he continued to provide ammunition to the forces lining up against him. In this case it had to do with the town constables. As previously mentioned, constables and deputy sheriffs were the primary source of law enforcement before the formation of a police force at Coney Island, but under Chief of Police McKane the position of constable had evolved into a position of political patronage.

Gravesend constables made such a good living with their questionable billing practices that the population of Gravesend began to tire of the increased taxes caused mainly by the bills submitted by the town's four constables. McKane knew he had to do something to placate the people, so in 1889 he attempted to have the charges billed by Gravesend constables made the responsibility of the county to pay. In this way, McKane tried to look like the people's champion by having the responsibility switched to the county, but he didn't think about county officials scrutinizing the bills. The first county official to come at McKane was District Attorney James Ridgeway, who already had an ax to grind with McKane over the heat he received from Anthony Comstock. Ridgeway made the following statement regarding the Gravesend constables:

"They had a police force in Coney Island and three or four constables. In the summer when the bummers go to the seashore to cool off, the policemen arrest them and hide them away until night and then call the constable. He turns the prisoner over to the constable who takes credit for the arrest. He takes them to court and prefers charges against them, usually for vagrancy or intoxication – 90% of the charges are discharged. Then the constable submits a bill to the county. He charges so much for a warrant as if a warrant had been issued, so much for serving, so much for mileage, so much for a recall and so much for a subpoena. His charge goes through the old statutory fee bill. That is a transparent fraud and costs the county up

to $8000 a year. Just think of it. A Chief Justice makes $8000 and now a Gravesend constable is making as much."[42]

County Supervisor William A. Watson had been unsuccessful in his bid to be elected Assemblyman, mainly due to the fact that John McKane had thrown his support behind the other candidate. Watson held a grudge against McKane so when investigative hearings were conducted regarding the billing practices of the Gravesend constables, Watson attacked.

Ex-Assemblyman John J. Kurth, the man who had presented Captain Hinman with his gold shield, was on hand to speak for a bill to increase the size of the Gravesend police force. He began by saying Gravesend had a population of 10,000, but during the summer the population swelled to near 100,000. Kurth said they had only 16 policemen in the town, which was inadequate during the summer season. Kurth went on to say that the Kings County Board of Supervisors had recently raised objections to the bills charged by Gravesend constables, but that if the bill to increase the police to 26 was passed more arrests would be made by the police, reducing the constable's bills.

William Watson sprung to the attack. "Who makes the arrests now in Gravesend?"

"The constables make nearly all the arrests," said Kurth.

"How many constables are there?"

"Four."

Watson smiled. "Well, if four constables at present do more work than your sixteen policemen, I can't see the use in increasing such a force, unless you are suggesting that the laziness of the police force is due to the fact that the constables work on a fee basis while the police officers draw a regular salary."

Mr. Watson said the supervisors committee appointed to investigate the Gravesend police had taken testimony that showed the members of the police department usually acted as runners for the four constables, turning over prisoners to them so they might collect fees. He said, "If McKane is granted more police, the number of runners for the constables will be increased. The Gravesend constables make $5000 to $7000 a year."

Watson's statement prompted one committee member to say he wished he could become a constable. Watson agreed and said the large constable fees were due to the fact that they charged mileage for transporting prisoners from the hallway at the courthouse to the courtroom after receiving the prisoners from the police. They might take a prisoner into the next room and charge a mile for it. Watson summed up with a proposition. "Would it not be better to abolish the police and hire four more constables?"

The County Board of Supervisors ended up rejecting the constable's bills, especially when one bill reflected that a constable travelled 625 miles in five days.[43]

John McKane kept a firm grasp on power in Gravesend despite the investigations and allegations piling up against him and his police force. One of the main reasons for his apparent Teflon persona was the firm support he received from the Democratic party. McKane seemed to be immune and unconcerned about the investigations closing in on him. At a testimonial dinner, attended by 1,000 loyalists held in West Brighton at Bauer's Casino, the highlight of the gaudy event was the presentation of a breast shield to the "Chief." The shield was described as follows:

A gold badge with a diamond star within a circle, and upon it enameled, Chief of Police, Gravesend, Long Island; a laurel wreath worked in diamonds and emeralds surmounted with an eagle with outstretched wings set in diamonds; on the back was engraved, "Presented to the Honorable John McKane by his friends at Paul Bauer's Casino, Coney Island. Veritas Vincit." The badge held 229 brilliants and 110 emeralds.

Ironically, Veritas Vincit, translates to "TRUTH PREVAILS."

McKane also issued new police shields to the regular and special officers of Gravesend. The regular officers were provided with a gold-plated shield surrounded by an eagle and the words "Gravesend Police," together with the number of the badge on the face of the shield. The design for the special officers' shield was the same, but the shield was silver.

By the mid-1890s Coney Island looked like this

The Ablemarle Hotel – John McKane's unofficial police

headquarters where he would sit on the veranda and watch the crowd on Surf Avenue.

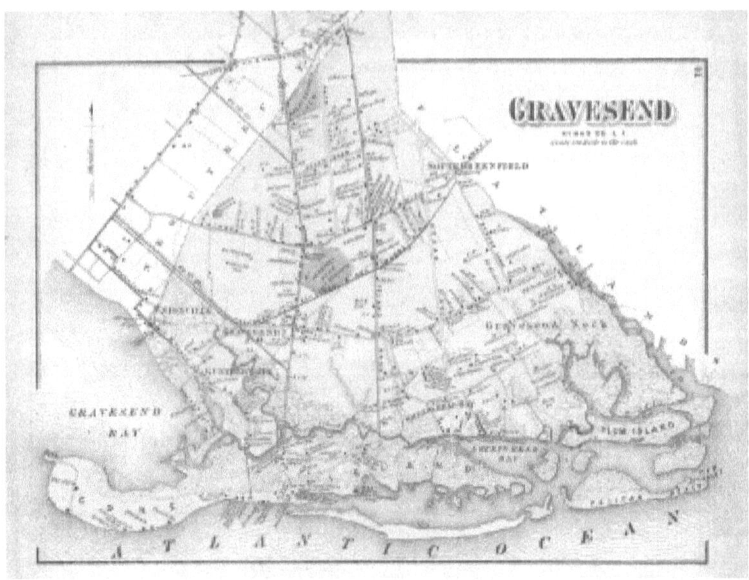

Police Officer patrols Steeplechase Park as camel ride passes

THE STAB IN THE BACK

In 1887 the first big step in the downfall of John McKane occurred. The cause depended on one's perspective. It might have been McKane's thirst for undisputed rule of his town, or maybe it was the simple case of a man who wanted to do the honorable thing by fulfilling a promise.

In 1886 McKane, a member of the Democratic State Committee, recognized that his choice for Assemblyman in Gravesend, Richard V.B. Newtown, was in a very tough fight against his Republican opponent. McKane reached out to Cornelius Ferguson, Supervisor of New Utrecht, for support, and with the promise of reciprocal support in a future election, Ferguson's support helped to secure Newton's victory.

A year later Ferguson cashed in on McKane's promise by asking for his support for Daniel W. Tallmadge for the Assembly. The request was straightforward and not unexpected. What was totally unexpected, however, was the fact that New Utrecht was backing a Republican.

On one hand, a Republican representative in the Legislature who owed his election to McKane would be more useful in preventing adverse legislation than would be a Democrat regardless of how treacherous the act would be perceived by the Democratic establishment. On the other hand, a promise was a promise, and McKane's promise of support had not been contingent on a specific political party.[44]

Whatever the specific reason was for McKane's support, the result was an extraordinary change in the votes of the county towns of Gravesend and New Utrecht and the State and Assembly tickets. McKane was roundly abused by Democrats for the practically unanimous vote which Mr. Daniel W. Tallmadge, the Republican candidate for the assembly in the twelfth District, received in Gravesend, while Mr. Benedict, the Democratic candidate received the normal vote of the town.[45]

There were immediate calls for McKane's head within the Democratic party because of his treachery, but the expressive wrath of the 26th Ward relative to the slaughter of Democratic candidate Benedict seemed to quickly settle down. In the first place McKane and his co-conspirator, Ferguson, of New Utrecht were bad men to tackle. Each was entrenched behind 700 or 800 votes, the aggressive use of which might prove unfortunate in state and county elections. The better strategy for wrathful 26th Warders was to not make a fuss over an Assemblyman, but to load themselves up for future vengeance.[46]

For McKane's part, he made a brief statement before the Democratic Committee attempting to explain his action.

"As you know, I have voted the Democratic ticket ever since I have voted and I voted it on the last election day with one exception, and that was for the assembly. I say this without any remorse that I came here merely to explain that I kept my word with a friend, and I must say that it would have been better, perhaps for me, politically, if I had broken my word. But it is something I have never done in my life. If I did any harm or if it will be productive of harm, I am willing to take my censure, whatever it may be. I want to say that the Association of the Town of Gravesend did everything in their power to get me to stop. The President of the association begged me to stop, and I do not think it is manly for me to sit here and hear him abused. The only man to blame in the town is John Y. McKane for the majority he got. I expect to take my medicine. I bid you goodnight." [47]

It didn't take long for the political score to be settled. The hardliners in the Brooklyn Democratic machine were determined to sacrifice McKane by kicking him out of the party. It looked as though the wheels of the great juggernaut of the machine were being oiled especially for the annihilation not only of the Gravesend rebel, but of those who had friendly sentiments for him. Whether certain gentlemen would elect to go down with a sinking ship or desert it before it was submerged, would be known before long. They would be admired if they stood by their colors, but they risked being ruined if they did not turn on McKane. There was not the least doubt, however, as to the party wisdom of the whole disciplinary movement. They could not permit treachery to go unpunished simply because the traitor was a man of prominence and power. That would establish a precedent likely to result in nothing but disintegration. Every ward leader with a little grievance would follow the illustrious example of McKane and plead the immunity granted him as justifying clemency in their own case.[48]

John McKane addressed his discipline with the following statement.

"I have been in the Democratic party for 25-years and if my recent action was a mistake it is the first one I have made. I am not sorry for what I have done and would do the same thing over again. I have gone on the plan through life to keep my word and I think that my promise in politics should be worth as much as my promise in business. I am a Democrat now as I have always been and there is no man in the party that would do more for its success than I."[49]

With that, McKane shrugged and along with all his supporters in Gravesend, he switched to the Republican party.

Depiction of 1872 Coney Island beach scene

THE INCIDENT

McKane somehow managed to avoid conviction throughout the 1880s despite several attempts by the New York State Legislature. His luck finally ran out during the 1893 election cycle when he refused to turn clearly phony voting tallies over to the Brooklyn Supreme Court. By that time McKane had become an impediment to the island's growth. The New York Times declared that Coney Island had become Sodom by the Sea, and worried that its reputation would keep people away. That year, to keep a reform candidate out of office McKane registered 6,218 voters, 5,000 more that Coney Island's entire eligible voting population.[50]

McKane's police officers took the names of any male visitor old enough to vote and used them to forge the Gravesend's voter registry. This system relied on threats: seasonal workers were reminded (forcefully) that if they failed to vote on Election Day, they would not have a job at Coney Island the following summer. Visitors were threatened with arrest if they refused to turn over their names to the police. McKane even paid to import voters by train from nearby jurisdictions each Election Day. He moved the polls to Town Hall where his cronies could exert complete control over every man who walked in to vote. His methods worked, helping him to maintain political control and become a wealthy man. By 1893, he had been Coney's ostensible ruler for over twelve years. The Gravesend voter lists were fully loaded with names of non-residents, the deceased, and fake persons in preparation for Election Day. The Times had previously tried to expose McKane's illegal methods and voter fraud, but the State of New York had never mounted a successful challenge to his control there. The state legislature previously had passed an election reform bill that was designed to stop McKane's practice of sitting in the Town Hall where he could eye each voter. The law stipulated a separate polling place for each of Gravesend's six districts. However, McKane flaunted the law by redistricting the town so that each ended with a ribbon of land that led into the seventy-eight by thirty-seven- foot Town Hall via six doors.

In November of 1893 McKane received a warning that a group of Republican reformers were planning to observe the election in Gravesend. Naturally McKane wasn't going to let it happen and instructed 150 of his henchmen armed with clubs to make sure that no strangers approached the Town Hall. He was particularly worried because of all the fraudulent votes he had registered in all six districts.

Three carriages filled with strangers approached the Town Hall at sunrise and were met by a hostile crowd of 300 men, led by fifty policemen. The reformer's leader was Colonel Alexander Bacon, the same man who five years earlier headed the committee attempting to expose McKane's corruption. The Colonel and a dozen or more lawyers, physicians, merchants and clergymen had come armed with an injunction from Judge Barnard to lawfully observe the election and make sure it was honest. When the Colonel told McKane that he had an injunction for him, McKane with his hands firmly clasped behind his back, confidently proclaimed, "Injunctions don't go here."

Bacon held out the paper and lunged forward to serve it by slapping him with it on the chest and shoulders. McKane, as arrogant as ever, arrested them but not before McKane's men shoved and pushed them, knocking them down and even hitting the men with their nightsticks. They were arrested for disturbing the peace and put in a cell. McKane celebrated his latest triumph and opened the polls.

One stranger escaped, and the story was carried back to the editor of the Brooklyn Eagle. By noon he printed a special edition about the incident at Coney Island with the headline "Injunctions Don't Go Here!". The wire services picked up the story and by the end of the day the entire country was reading about it.

Based on his past successes, McKane was confident that the incident would blow over in a day or two like all the rest. However, reformers swept into office both in the State Supreme Court, State

Attorney General's Office and in the Mayor's Office of nearby Brooklyn. Worse for McKane, the reformers were howling for blood. Newly appointed assistant attorney generals summoned an extraordinary grand jury into session.

On December 31st the extraordinary grand jury handed up its indictments. There were eleven counts against McKane, two of his lieutenants, and eighteen prominent citizens of Coney Island who served as election officials. McKane was the only one required to stand before the bench to answer the indictments. He thought his friends would turn up and bail him out of trouble, but he was wrong.

The trial began on January 23, 1894, in the old Brooklyn Supreme Court House. Specifically, Part II of the Supreme Court was the theatre of the trial of John Y. McKane and his Gravesend associates charged with contempt of court. E.M. Shepard, who appeared as Deputy Attorney General, and Colonel A.E. Lamb with E.M. Grout were seated together in one group at the lawyer's table. They were the prosecuting counsel. Judge James Troy, General I.S. Catlin and George W. Roderick were in another group at the same table and appeared to defend McKane and the other defendants.

The courtroom was packed with McKane's friends and sympathizers who didn't understand why their leader was being prosecuted. They thought that stealing votes was the normal state of affairs. Besides, McKane always looked the other way and permitted innocent gambling at the horse racing tracks, sanctioned prize fighting and ignored Sunday Blue Laws. In short, they felt that Coney Island's way of life was on trial.

The testimony at the trial, besides providing damning evidence against McKane, provided some amazing insights into the police operations at Coney Island. Captain Hinman astonished the judge with his ignorance of the knowledge of the men under his command. He testified that John McKane was the chief of police and that he and Garretson Morris were captains, and that Morris had the Sheepshead

Bay district while he had the Coney Island district. Hinman further testified that Louis Potter, William Van Fricken, Michael Murphy, and Morton Morris were the sergeants working under him, but he did not know the names of the sergeants under Captain Morris. Hinman said he met with McKane once a day at the Coney Island police headquarters, sometimes for five minutes and sometimes for over an hour. When asked about the police in the villages of Greenfield, Gravesend and Sheepshead Bay Hinman testified as follows:

A.- I don't know how many men they have in the town of Gravesend.

Q. - What do you mean by "they?"

A. - The Police Board.

Q. – These are the men under you, bound to obey your orders?

A. – Yes, sir.

Q. – And you don't know how many there are?

A. – No, sir. (laughter in courtroom).

"That's the most remarkable statement I ever heard," cried the judge.

Captain Hinman had no idea how many men there were on the force during the winter in Sheepshead Bay. He thought there were about four men on duty in Gravesend Beach. He said they did not report to him, and he did not know who they reported to.

Again, the judge interrupted the witness in astonishment. "You are a captain of police and don't know?"

"No, sir," Hinman admitted. Again, laughter filled the courtroom.

The captain also acknowledged he did not know the badge numbers of his policemen.

"Do you know the number of a single policeman?" the judge asked severely.

"No, sir." (laughter).

The captain also said he did not know who assigned the badge numbers to the Gravesend policemen.

The judge began a follow-up question. "What use are the numbers?" Before Hinman could respond the judge answered his own question. "Evidently, not much use." The laughter in the courtroom continued.

Captain Hinman attempted to answer the question anyway by saying that if a citizen made a complaint against a policeman, he would take his badge number.

The judge threw his arms out to the side. "What good is that if the captain doesn't know the badge numbers of his men?" There was now more laughter in the courtroom than quiet moments.

Captain Hinman said he and the four sergeants were on duty all year round, and that he assumed the Police Board appointed policemen, but he wasn't sure, and he didn't know who issued badges with numbers, but again assumed it was a member of the Police Board. He explained that he knew his men by name and not by badge number.[51]

Captain Hinman's testimony also revealed that he was paid his police salary by personal check from John McKane - $2.50 a day – with no set pay day. He said that whenever he needed money he went to McKane and asked for his pay, and that he didn't know how other members of department were paid.[52]

Regarding the Election Day incident, Captain Hinman testified that he was in command of the police in Gravesend and that there was considerable excitement preceding the election owing to the presence of non-resident drunken men and as more excitement was expected on Election Day, he telephoned Chief McKane for instructions. He was told to have his men on hand but not to use violence. On election morning he saw several carriages and he met with the chief at the Heirlein's Hotel. Shortly after he saw several men scuffling around the booths; they were armed with sticks and when McKane approached Hinman heard someone shout "Come on, here he is!" Hinman saw no blows struck by any of his officers nor did he see any injunction served that day. He said some men were arrested for creating a disturbance.[53]

The election watchers testified, and while it was damming, it might not have convinced the jury. Then they asked McKane if he had ever actually seen the voter registration lists. He stated under oath that he had definitely never inspected them. That was a big mistake because the Special Attorney General, Benjamin Tracy, pulled out McKane's own affidavit, in which he had sworn only two months earlier that he personally inspected all Gravesend's registration lists. McKane flushed deep brick-red. The gavel banged and the court adjourned for the weekend.

When McKane took the stand on Monday he was again caught in a web of his own lies. It was established that the Coney Island policemen that attacked the poll watchers, like Captain Hinman, were paid by checks drawn on McKane's personal bank account, and that he padded the voter registration rolls by more than 200% in three years. After a six-hour impassioned summation, Tracy rested his case. Now it would be up to the jury.

When the jury didn't reach a verdict the first day, it was speculated that at least three of the jurors had been bribed to hold out for McKane's acquittal. The following afternoon the jury reached its verdict. Everyone filed back into court, but they had to wait ten minutes before McKane arrived. The jury filed in, and the foreman of the jury stood to read the verdict. "Guilty," said the foreman. McKane stared unbelieving, for he was sure that at least one of the three jurors that he offered a house and land to, would take the bribe.

McKane was also sure that he would somehow elude punishment. There were even rumors that his Coney Island gang planned to raid the jail and whisk him off to Cuba. But on Monday, February 19th he was sentenced to six years in the Sing Sing State Penitentiary, at hard labor. Crowds lined the Brooklyn streets to watch him being escorted to prison.

His lieutenants were also tried. Kenny Sutherland was found guilty, but he jumped bail and fled to Canada before he could be sentenced. Dick Newton turned state's evidence and pleaded guilty. Others pled guilty or turned state's evidence and were let off with relatively light sentences. McKane and his henchmen's political reign had ended.

Gravesend Town Hall – the scene of the Election Day incident that led to the
Downfall of John McKane.

Artist depiction of the Election Day incident.

THE AFTERMATH

John Y. McKane, the dethroned chieftain of Gravesend, started for the State Prison at Sing Sing at 12:05 PM. The Raymond Street jail and vicinity were crowded with people, many of them morbid curiosity seekers, but the great majority friends and acquaintances of the prisoner for many years. Some of them had been waiting for his departure since early morning and shifted uneasily from place to place as the noon hour approached. The little saloon which stood diagonally opposite the jail did a thriving business all through the morning, and the short, good-natured proprietor, who seemed to have watched the gray, gaunt walls of the prison day and night since McKane was incarcerated, entertained his patrons with stories of how Judge Newton hustled back and forth at all hours on errands for his political chief. McKane had hardly breakfasted when scores of people, nearly all of them Gravesenders, presented themselves at the door of the jail and asked admission.

No surprises were expected from McKane, who had been well behaved throughout, but the sheriff was taking no chances and turned out every man under him with instructions to keep their eyes open and their heads clear. At about 11:45 a coach was driven into the jail yard, which was a signal for the crowd to gather around the entrance. A squad of police were on hand, and in a few moments the driveway was cleared. At 12:02 the big gates swung open, and the coach dashed out and turned left. All the curtains were drawn so that it was impossible to see who was inside, but Sheriff Buttling informed the press that in addition to himself, keepers Wilson, Jameson, and Thompson accompanied McKane on his journey to Sing Sing.[54]

John T. Hinman had managed to avoid prison, but his days as a police captain were over. Since McKane and the other captain, Garretson Morris, were in prison, the Police Board met to appoint a new Chief of Police.[55]

The Police Board of Gravesend appointed James A. Eustis to succeed John McKane as Chief of Police. Eustis, 38 years old, was in the grocery business in Coney Island and was a prominent member of the Citizen's league.[56]

The most pressing issue for the new chief was a report submitted by Police Justice Gladding showing that back pay owed to Coney Island policemen was not less than $25,000, with a chance that it would be a great deal more. The report was a fair illustration of the methods that prevailed at Coney Island under McKane management. Not a single policeman on the force was paid a salary weekly, monthly, or annually. Each man went to McKane and obtained money from him on account. He paid everybody in part but nobody in full. The loyalty of which his followers had boasted of was a loyalty born of necessity and not of admiration. Indeed, the officers under McKane were treated like dogs in the sense that they had to wait until he saw fit to throw them a bone for the support of themselves and their families.[57]

The tenure of James Eustis as Chief of Police lasted less than a month. On April 26, 1894, a bill passed in the New York State Legislature that annexed Gravesend and Coney Island to Brooklyn. With the stroke of a pen the Gravesend Police Department ceased to exist, and policing Coney Island became the responsibility of the Brooklyn Police Department.

On May 6, 1894, Inspector McKelvey, of the Brooklyn Police Department, went to Gravesend with a contingent of Brooklyn officers and took charge of the place. Brooklyn Police Commissioner Welles accompanied McKelvey and said that as the Gravesend Police were legislated out of office by the bill incorporating that town into Brooklyn, that he would probably make some selections from the old force, but only the best men would be selected. He further stated that the Coney Island Police headquarters would be used temporarily as the new station house known as the Twenty Fourth Precinct.[58]

McKelvey and Welles had a very interesting meeting with the new and soon to be former Chief of Police Eustis. When they asked Eustis for a complete list of the members of the Gravesend Police Department, Eustis shocked the Brooklyn lawmen when he said such a list did not exist. Eustis further stated that as far as he knew there were no police department records or desk blotter. The only record Eustis could provide was a handwritten piece of paper on which 26 patrol posts were crudely drawn.

Inspector McKelvey relieved Eustis of his position and appointed Sergeant Elias Clayton as the commanding officer of the new Twenty-Fourth Precinct. Along with the new commander came 42 experienced patrolmen assigned from precincts all over the city.[59]

The first installment of the police in the Brooklyn uniform arrived at 8 AM on May 6th. There were ten in the squad, and they marched boldly to the John McKane holy of holies, the rattle-trapped frame Police Headquarters. Soon they were followed by others. The Gravesenders watched them as conquered people watch the enemy descend upon them with flame and sword. In all 42 policemen came down on the cars and two sergeants. Soon after, six mounted policemen, under the command of a sergeant appeared. Before 9 AM the twenty-fourth police precinct of Brooklyn was organized under the command of Sergeant E.P. Clayton, who made John McKane's former private office his own.

The first thing Acting Captain Clayton did was to detail twenty patrolmen to visit every place in West Brighton and inform the proprietors that no open violation of the law would be permitted. They were told that they were to do nothing that could not be done in the city of Brooklyn. The saloons were to be closed and the sacred concerts allowed only so long as they were such within the meaning of the law. No one would be allowed to go upon the stage in costume or in character.

It was only a little while after the policemen had made their rounds that the performers and musicians began to appear. This early in the season they were engaged for Sundays only. Some of the musicians who had arrived earlier in the day were sent back to the city wearing very disgusted expressions.[60]

As time passed, the former members of the Gravesend Police Department began besieging the police headquarters. The men who were formerly on the police force under the town government were looking for a fresh chance in the city, and the first batch of 25, including several sergeants came up to take the physical examination that was a prerequisite for appointment. If they got through that alright, they were excused from further examination as to their qualities. They were hopeful that at least 70 men would get positions on the force.[61]

Prison crushed McKane's spirit. He refused to allow his wife or children to visit him because he didn't want to be seen in prison stripes. Besides receiving no visitors, he had no real friends among the inmates. McKane was released two years early for good behavior from prison on April 30, 1898. He returned to Coney Island, but all had changed. He was old and embittered and his friends were gone. He began selling life insurance policies to keep busy. He didn't need the money; there were plenty of mortgages that were in his wife's name.

McKane had returned to a completely different Brooklyn. On January 1, 1898, Brooklyn was consolidated into the Greater City of New York. Brooklyn was no longer a great city but had become one of five boroughs within the City of New York. McKane's former police department had changed too. The men policing Coney Island were no longer members of a Brooklyn Police Department but were instead members of the New York City Police Department.

McKane died several months after a stroke in 1899. He was 58 years old and had been out of prison for just one year. The closest family members of his well-attended funeral were his wife, brother, and a blind daughter. Whatever faults McKane may have had, it cannot be argued that during his time in power, John McKane was the most important figure in law enforcement in Coney Island.

Typical Coney Island beach crowd.

John McKane being taken to jail after conviction

LEGACIES

The demise of John McKane was not the end of the early era of policing in Coney Island. Legacies involving the "special policemen" continued to exist and continue to function in the present day.

During the reign of John McKane, he encouraged different railroads and trolley lines to service Coney Island. The more accessible Coney Island became the more people could travel to the boss's playground to spend their money on amusements and gambling.

Most of the police operating in Coney Island were not from the Gravesend town force – they were special officers appointed by Chief of Police McKane, but employed and paid by the hotels, racetracks and other Coney Island businesses, including the rail lines.

In 1894 Gravesend was annexed by the City of Brooklyn and it became the responsibility of the Brooklyn Police Department to appoint special policemen. On January 19th, 1896, papers were filed to incorporate the Brooklyn Rapid Transit Corporation (the BRT). The BRT was not an operator, simply a holding company set up to acquire the properties of the other transit interests. Shortly after incorporating, the BRT began a campaign of acquisition of various streetcar, elevated and steam railroads. By 1900, the BRT had taken over the Sea Beach Railway. In 1899, the Nassau Electric Railway, which took over the Brighton Beach &Coney Island Railway, was taken under BRT control. The Brooklyn Elevated and Union Elevated Railways were consolidated into the Brooklyn Union Elevated Railroad Company in that same year. In fact, in1900, most of the Brooklyn railroads were in financial straits, and the BRT simply gobbled them up. By the end of 1900, every Brooklyn line was under BRT control, except the Brooklyn and Rockaway Beach Railroad, which didn't fall under BRT control until 1906.

In 1898 Brooklyn was consolidated into the Greater City of New York, making the Commissioner of the New York City Police

Department responsible for appointing special police officers, including those special officers working for the BRT.

August 12, 1906, saw such jaw-dropping chaos in Brooklyn that our present-day gripes about public transportation would wither and die by comparison. But the story did not begin on the 12th. It was on July 24th that Dr. T.J. MacFarlane was making a routine trip on the Culver Line from Coney Island to Downton Brooklyn. Dr. MacFarlane paid the five-cent fare when he boarded at Coney Island, but he was shocked when the car passed Kings Highway and the conductor demanded another five cents due to the company's new "double fare" policy. MacFarlane refused to pay the second fare and also refused the conductor's order to leave the car. Shortly thereafter a special police officer placed MacFarlane under arrest.

As soon as he was released, Dr. MacFarlane filed a lawsuit against the BRT, and Justice Gaynor of the Appellate Division of the Supreme Court ruled that the railroads could not charge a double fare for one continuous trip. Despite Gaynor's ruling, the BRT demanded a second nickel from trolley riders once they passed Kings Highway on the various lines it controlled: the Sea Beach Railway, the Brighton Line, and Culver Line. The BRT's uniformed special police force ejected every passenger who refused to pay. With hundreds–maybe thousands–of riders out on the street, swarming the tracks, the cars could not move and did not move.

August 12th was a day of violence on the Coney Island surface cars and elevated trains. The disturbances that began over the refusal of many passengers to pay a double fare to Coney Island, were exasperated as more and more people became aware of Judge Gaynor's ruling. More than 250,000 people started out for Coney Island, and it was estimated that 2,000 were thrown from the cars by 250 special policemen. The most serious incident of the day was the flinging of three people into Coney Island Creek from a moving car. Men were clubbed and thrown off the cars with alarming frequency, and one special officer threw a man off a car and then he grabbed the man's two-year old baby, which had been sitting beside him, and yanked him into the dust of the road.[62] It was also reported that the BRT had set up a "bull pen" in Coney Island where riders were detained until they paid the second fare.[63]

Brooklyn Borough President Bird Coler was outraged at the behavior of the BRT and its police force. He made a vigorous complaint to the New York City Police Department which resulted in Deputy Police Commissioner Arthur O'Keeffe's visit to Brooklyn. O'Keeffe conducted his investigation by visiting the various second fare points where the inspectors and special policemen committed brutal assaults upon passengers and threw them from cars. After completing his inquiry O'Keeffe announced that the licenses of all BRT special policemen were revoked.

Vice President and General Manager of the BRT, John F. Calderwood, disregarded O'Keeffe's announcement and said that the BRT intended to do business in the same old way and would collect ten cent fare to and from Coney Island.

Deputy Commissioner O'Keeffe quickly fired off the following letter to Acting Police Commissioner Rhinelander Waldo:

Dear Sir: On Sunday, August 12th, 1906, I witnessed cases of assault by the special officers of the B.R.T. who wear a uniform similar to that of the regular force. These men acted in a lawless manner and in defiance of public policy. I would respectfully recommend that all these men be forced to change their uniforms. I also recommend that the appointment of every special officer employed by the B.R.T. company be revoked until an investigation can be held to ascertain their fitness and ability to act as special guardians of the peace.

Upon receiving a quick response from Waldo, O'Keeffe sent the following letter to Calderwood:

Sir: I am empowered by the acting police commissioner to notify you herewith that the appointments of all special patrolmen for your company have been revoked, to take effect at 6 o'clock this P.M.

Any of said special patrolmen found exercising the powers of special officers after that hour make themselves amenable to arrest on the charge of impersonating a police officer.

The acting police commissioner further directs that permission given by this department allowing special officers in your employ to wear uniforms other than that prescribed for special patrolmen (which is a gray uniform) is likewise revoked.[64]

In the meantime, Borough President Bird Coler Called upon Sheriff M.J. Flaherty to swear in special deputy sheriffs to take hold of the situation and preserve the peace and protect passengers from assault at the hands of employees of the railroad companies. But the special deputies never materialized. [65]

The unintended result of the removal of the special police was the rejoicing among criminal circles. The knowledge that the railroad held a force of over two hundred trained police at all times for protection of its property and patrons had been a deterrent to this element. When the news came that this bar had been removed there was joy among the pickpockets and thugs, as well as the simpler classes of troublemakers who kept busy along the trolley lines.

Until their shields were taken from them, the BRT police made their regular beats up and down the elevated lines through the town, and the knowledge that they would regularly appear at each point along the system had its moral effect.[66]

On September 7th, 1906 BRT General Manager John Calderwood sounded the death knell for the special police in the following communication to Heads of BRT Departments:

On account of the revocation by the municipal police authorities of appointments of our special officers, the force heretofore employed under the superintendent of employment and inspection, in the maintenance of order on cars and trains and about the company's property and in the protection of our patrons, will be disbanded this date.

Until further notice, where the services of police officers are required, you will notify police headquarters, Borough of Brooklyn (Telephone 7000 Main).

This information is being sent because the company has determined to give up the matter and let the question of disorder on its cars settle itself. There has been no lessening in the complaints of crime and disorder, it simply has reached the point where, denied the privilege of hiring a police force at its own expense to do the work that as a taxpayer should be done for it by the city, it throws up its hands.

We are most reluctant to turn out of positions a body of men who have worked both steadily and faithfully. Yet, the possibility of our force ever regaining its shields is so uncertain as to keep us from feeling warranted in keeping these men longer in our service.[67]

The special police never did come back. As time went on, the BRT got cocky and adapted a "public be damned" attitude, with poor customer relationship management techniques. The company deteriorated further with a strike in late October 1918. As a result of pressing untrained motormen into service to cover the striking workers, the worst accident to befall rapid transit in New York City, the Malbone Street wreck, occurred on November 1st, 1918, where at least 93 people lost their lives. This was the proverbial "straw that broke the camel's back," and the company went into bankruptcy shortly thereafter. It remained in receivership until 1923, when it was reorganized as the Brooklyn-Manhattan Transit Corporation, or the BMT.

The BMT brought with it a change in attitude, but the political winds in New York City were changing, and "Unification" was "the word". After several City administrations and financial troubles, in June of 1940, the BMT lost its identity as a corporate entity and became, simply, the BMT Division of the New York City Rapid Transit System.

On November 17,1933 the special police returned when six men were sworn in as New York State Railway Police. They were unarmed but were still responsible for the safety of the passengers on the IND as well as guarding property. Two years later, twenty station supervisors were added for police duty. Responsible for assisting in the opening and closing of doors and announcing destinations, these 26 special police were soon given powers of arrest, but only on the IND line. In 1937, 160 more men were added to this police force. Additionally, 3 lieutenants, 1 captain, and 1 inspector from the NYPD were assigned as supervisors. When the privately run IRT and BMT were taken over by New York City in 1940, the small patrol force on the IND line nearly doubled in size. Now part of the Civil Service system, more transit supervisors were needed. In 1942, the first promotional exam was given for the title of "special patrolman grade 2" – or what is now known as a sergeant.

The Code of Criminal Procedure was changed in 1947 granting these transit patrolmen peace officer status and by 1950, the number of special policemen reached 563. The following year, exams were held for both transit sergeants and lieutenants. In 1953, the New York City Transit Authority came into being and assumed control over all the subway lines. The special policemen officially became the Transit Police Department and remained an independent police force in New York City until being merged into the NYPD in 1995.

Another legacy to the special police still exists on Coney Island. On a city map, nothing separates the neighborhood of Coney Island from the private community of Sea Gate. The gated area is on the western edge of the peninsula in Southern Brooklyn that Coney Island sits on. But at West 37th street's intersections with Surf and Mermaid Avenues, roadblocks housed by brick and metal gates manned by Sea Gate policemen completely close Sea Gate off from the rest of Coney Island.

The Town of Gravesend consisted of the areas of Coney Island, Brighton Beach, Sheepshead Bay, Manhattan Beach, and Sea Gate. To a degree, the legacy of policing at Coney Island before the NYPD is still alive at Sea Gate. To understand Sea Gate's unique policing situation, one must first know some of the history of the area.

Sea Gate is a virtual city within a city. For while Sea Gate is part of the borough of Brooklyn in New York City, it is also by virtue of a peculiar and rather interesting development, a municipal unit by itself, with its own system of public utilities, its own mode of taxation, and its own standards of law and order enforceable by communal authority, in addition to those imposed by the laws of the city and state.

This land at the western tip of Coney Island is itself an ancient lineage, for it was granted in part by the Dutch and Danish governments to the settlers of the old Town of Gravesend and in part by the Native Americans. Practically useless for the purposes of cultivation and for residence in those early years, unsupplied as it was of water or with easy communication to the mainland, it drifted in the course of time into the common lands of the town, there to remain until our hero John McKane, in the generous fashion that he had, sold it at bargain rates to some of his friends and pocketed the proceeds. McKane did the same with a lot of Coney Island during his reign over the town. The chances he took were of going to prison, where he eventually landed. The chances his friends took were of having their cheaply bought lands taken away from them when it was found that McKane did not record the passing of title because he didn't want his fraud discovered.

Sea Gate was formerly known as Norton's Point, and the peculiarity about the conditions under which a good part this territory was owned led to almost endless litigation when, in the later days when there was a water supply and electric trolleys, people undertook to develop the land for residential purposes. But eventually, the difficulties in the title situation were cleared away, and Norton's Point Land

Company took over the property and began to lay it out. Like all similar undertakings, it was slow business. In 1896 there were hardly a half dozen cottages at Sea Gate. In 1901 there were perhaps fifty. In 1906 there were 150 homes and the Atlantic Yacht Club at Sea Gate.

The idea of a communal government for Sea Gate came to the minds of several New York businessmen who had settled there, and it took definite shape in 1899 when the Sea Gate Association was incorporated. The natural lay of the land strongly favored the scheme, for as the property of the Norton's Point Land Company was at the extreme end of the point, with water on three sides and a land approach only on one, it was beyond possibility the city should ever require a right of way through it for any public purpose.

So when the streets were laid out and paved inside the big picket fence; when water pipes were put in and the various other utilities developed that were required for habitation, the settlement remained in the eyes of the law just as much private property, highways and all, as when it was acquired by the land improvement company, a dismal stretch of rolling sand dunes washed by the ocean surf on the one side and more gently caressed by the waters of Gravesend Bay on the other. The fundamental proposition of the Sea Gate Association was to preserve this condition of private ownership, and then to see what could be achieved in the shape of communal government in which the rights of all property owners would be recognized and residents not property owners treated on exactly the same basis as in any city or town.

It took a couple of years to work things out, and it was not until January 1, 1901 that the Norton's Point Land Company deeded to the Sea Gate Association the land required for streets and other public purposes together with certain building lots, subject to rigid restrictions as to nuisance and objectionable industries.

Having acquired the public property of the place the next problem before the Sea Gate Association was to determine a basis of membership and at the same time a basis of control. It was eventually decided that every owner of one lot of land could belong to the association by paying the dues assessed upon members. And as the association controlled water, sewage, and lighting utilities, its membership became an essential of residence.

The community has its own police and street cleaning departments, the police, to be sure, wearing the uniform similar to the city of New York, but receiving their orders from the Sea Gate Association.[68]

Sea Gate has one of the most unusual police systems within any large city in America. Sea Gate's police force is distinctive in that it is a force within a force, that is to say it is operative as a deputy police force employed by a corporation. The Sea Gate Association Inc. has the right to keep intruders from entering the "Gate." To do this they decided a police force is necessary, not only to keep intruders out but to preserve order within the restricted area. The reason that the public can be barred from Sea Gate is that the community operates under a charter from the State that it has legal recognition from the State as an organization. In line with this charter the Sea Gate Association, which is in itself unusual, maintains a police force which it hires and fires itself. This force operates in its duties independently of the NYPD and does not have to call on it unless assistance is required inside the gated community.

The Sea Gate Police Department patrols and protects Sea Gate's nearly 5,000 residents, who are predominantly Russian and orthodox Jewish. A large part of how they do that is by bottlenecking pedestrian and auto traffic into the community. It is an element of law enforcement separate from the New York City Police Department.

The Sea Gate Police Department was founded in 1899. It is a law enforcement agency made up of patrol officers, supervisors and a detective unit that investigates crimes that occur within Sea Gate's jurisdiction. The department answers to the Sea Gate Association and is funded by part of the annual dues that Seagate residents pay. The dues are 13 percent of the value of the resident's property.

There are 35 members of the SGPD. Eleven of those, including the Chief, are retired NYPD officers. The other 24 had no prior law enforcement experience, but all officers in the department have New York State peace officer powers and completed over one hundred hours of the New York State peace officer certification course spread over two months.

Sea Gate police officers have the same power as the NYPD within the community. They are authorized to make arrests, make car stops on Sea Gate property and issue summonses. They may carry a firearm, batons, pepper spray, and handcuffs. When an arrest is made, any on duty SGPD officer is able to take a suspect to the 60th Precinct, located on 8th street just north of Surf Avenue, for processing. While on duty they are fully sworn New York State peace officers.

There are many private gated communities in the Metropolitan Area, but Sea Gate is the only one with a police department. Before police purists blow a gasket, I realize Sea Gate is not a true "Police Department" in a legal sense, even though the entity is called the Sea Gate Police Department. As previously mentioned, the members of the department are peace officers, not police officers. Whereas police officers carry their police powers with them 24/7, the officers of Sea Gate have their sworn peace officer powers only when they are working at Sea Gate. Specifically, the officers of Sea Gate are designated New York City special patrolmen. The New York State Criminal Procedure Law defines all the titles within the state who are considered peace officers and #27 are New York City special patrolmen appointed by the police commissioner. Sea Gate officers carry firearms, but this is another difference between Sea Gate officers and the NYPD. Police officers carry firearms on the authority of their police officer status – no pistol permit is required. The special patrolmen at Sea Gate have to obtain a pistol permit in order to carry firearms while they are working.

Sea Gate officers are relics of a Coney Island long past, when politicians like John McKane ruled the land. They continue to prove their worth, however, by maintaining the dynamic of Sea Gate as a secure and private community on the edge on one of New York City's most underserved areas. The bottom line is that Sea Gate wouldn't be Sea Gate without the Sea Gate Police Department, and they also serve as a visible link to the special police of a bygone era of Coney Island.

Sea Gate today

Atlantic Yacht Club

Sea Gate Police patch circa 1899

Current patch

Sea Gate Police patrol vehicle

Sea Gate entrance

Sea Gate Police shield

Police muster in August 1906 to deploy for the "double-fare" violence

Police trying to handle crowd during "double-fare" violence

BROOKLYN'S SHIELDS

We have looked at many different law enforcement officers and agencies in the Coney Island area before the era of the NYPD. In closing, let's take a look at the shields worn by some of these officers in Coney Island and Brooklyn.

The shield, or badges of authority worn by police officers are an outcome of the devices embroidered on the coats, silverware, furniture, and horse trappings of knights of old. Coats of arms are supposed to have been first used at the German tournaments, finding their way later to England in the twelfth or thirteenth century. The custom was extended to the use of the national or family arms on seals.

The earliest account of wearing a badge goes back as far as 1122 when, it is said, Henry I placed around the neck of Geoffry of Anjou a shield adorned with small golden lions, on the latter's marriage to Henry's daughter. As the centuries rolled on the big feudal chiefs began to grant badges to their followers to serve as a means of recognition. They were then called cognizances and were displayed upon the coat.

When badges were first used by the police of American cities is not very clear, but the system has evidently been put in force wherever a regular police department has been organized. The first Brooklyn police shield was that worn by what was called the "Leatherhead" force, which was organized in 1840. On the back of the badge one end of a brass chain measuring about seven inches was soldered, the other end being furnished with a hook which was stuck in the policeman's coat. It was supposed that the chain would make the shield more secure, and this idea prevailed even after the consolidation of the Brooklyn Police into the New York City Police, but it was soon removed after a number of coats had been torn, through the chain catching on projections.

The first Brooklyn police shield was that worn by what was called the "Leatherhead" force, which was organized in 1840. On the back of the badge one end of a brass chain measuring about seven inches was soldered, the other end being furnished with a hook which was stuck in the policeman's coat. It was supposed that the chain would make the shield more secure, and this idea prevailed even after the consolidation of the Brooklyn Police into the New York City Police, but it was soon removed after a number of coats had been torn, through the chain catching on projections.

The above illustrations depict the various shields used by Kings County Deputy Sheriffs. The top shield is a very handsome badge issued to chief clerk and deputy sheriff Robert b. Sedgewick. It was made of solid gold with leaves on the side being of a greenish shade, probably Australian gold, which is much lighter in color than American gold. The lettering was in blue enamel. In the eye of the eagle was set a ruby. The arms of the state on new York were of unburnished gold and were set in a concave space. Surprisingly, there was no shield issued to the Sherriff, himself.

The above shields depict two of the badges used by the independent towns in Kings County before they were annexed to Brooklyn.

From 1857 – 1870 Brooklyn was part of the Metropolitan Police System. New York State created a Metropolitan Police District that included New York, Brooklyn, Richmond, and Westchester. All members of this new police district were under the control of New York State authorities, as opposed to the local municipalities. The aboveillustrations depict the tow styles of shields issued to the "Metropolitans". One style was distinguishable by an eagle on the top

In 1870 local control of police was re-established .The Brooklyn Police Department used the above shields. A Roundsman was a first level supervisor rank that was abolished early in the 20th century.

The post 1870 Sergeants and Captains shields were made more elaborately with the Captain being gold plated and the Sergeant painted black.

Post 1894 Brooklyn shields were used up until Brooklyn was consolidated into the Greater City of New York in 1898.

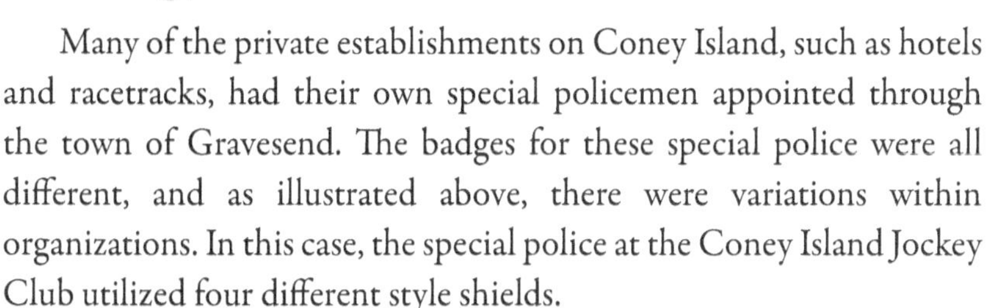

Many of the private establishments on Coney Island, such as hotels and racetracks, had their own special policemen appointed through the town of Gravesend. The badges for these special police were all different, and as illustrated above, there were variations within organizations. In this case, the special police at the Coney Island Jockey Club utilized four different style shields.

BIBLIOGRAPHY

1. McGerr, Michael, A Fierce Discontent: The Rise and Fall of the Progressive Movement in America (New York: Oxford University Press, 2003),

2. Rem Koolhaas, Delirious New York (New York: The Monacelli Press, Inc., 1994), 30. 2

3. McGerr, A Fierce Discontent, 27-35. 10 Ibid., 19. 5

4. THE HISTORY OF THE NEW YORK CITY POLICE DEPARTMENT, 1993

5. DESTROYING FENCES, The Brooklyn Daily Eagle, 4/26/1858, p3

6. UNTITLED, Kings County Rural Gazette, 7/29/1876, p2

7. A ROGUE ARRESTED, The Brooklyn Union, 8/11/1877, p3

8. UNTITLED, Kings County Rural Gazette, 7/29/1876, p2

9. METHODIST UNION PICNIC, Kings County Rural Gazette, 9/1/1877, p2

10. THE FIRST JAIL AT CONEY ISLAND, The Brooklyn Daily Eagle, 8/15/1877, p3

11. UNTITLED, The Brooklyn Daily Eagle, 4/3/1876, p4

12. Harold Coffin Syrett, The City of Brooklyn: 1865-1898 (New York: Columbia University Press, 1944), 185

13. THE COUNTY TOWN ELECTIONS, The Times Union, 4/3/1878, p4

14. FATE OF A CHOWDER PARTY, The Brooklyn Union, 9/3/1879, p2

15. FROM ALBANY, The Brooklyn Union, 6/9/1879, p4

16. SHERIFF STEGMAN'S APPOINTMENTS, The Brooklyn Daily Eagle, 6/9/1882, p4

17. UNTITLED, The Brooklyn Union, 6/23/1881, p3

18. "The Coney Island Gamblers," The New York Times, September 9, 1883.

19. A HARVEST OF WATCHES, The New York Times, 7/16/1888, p5
20. "The Pests of Coney Island," The New York Times, July 13, 1885. 52
21. FANCY FIGURES, The Brooklyn Daily Eagle, 3/19/1887, p4
22. AT WORK, The Brooklyn Daily Eagle, 9/27/1882, p2
23. UNTITLED, The Brooklyn Union, 6/23/1883, p6
24. POOL SELLING, The Brooklyn Union, 6/23/1883, p1
25. GENERAL CATLIN ON GAMBLING AT CONEY ISLAND, The Brooklyn Daily Eagle, 9/8/1883, p4
26. GAMBLING AT CONEY ISLAND, The Brooklyn Daily Eagle, 4/21/1884, p4
27. THE MAYOR AND THE POOL SELLERS, The Brooklyn Union, 5/12/1884, p2
28. OVER A CORPSE, The Brooklyn Union, 6/30/1884, p4
29. POLICE PROTECTION AT CONEY ISLAND, The Brooklyn Union, 6/21/1884, p4
30. UNTITLED, The Brooklyn Daily Eagle, 5/3/1885, p1
31. UNTITLED, The Brooklyn Daily Eagle, 7/5/1885, p8
32. CONEY ISLAND VAGRANTS RELEASED, The Brooklyn Union, 7/18/1885, p8
33. SUPERVISOR MCKANE'S AFFLICTION, The Brooklyn Union, 5/7/1885, p8
34. TWO ARRESTS, The Brooklyn Daily Eagle, 6/17/1886, p4
35. UNTITLED, The Brooklyn Union, 8/27/1886, p4
36. CHARGES FILED, The Brooklyn Daily Eagle, 9/11/1886, p6
37. UNTITLED, The Brooklyn Daily Eagle, 10/11/1886, p4
38. CONEY ISLAND'S POLICE STATION, The Brooklyn Daily Eagle, 5/30/1886, p1
39. CONEY ISLAND NEWS, The Brooklyn Union, 8/28/

1884, p4

40. AT A COCK FIGHT, The Brooklyn Daily Eagle, 7/21/.1886, p4

41. AT CONEY ISLAND, The Brooklyn Citizen, 5/26/1890, p2

42. RIDGEWAY REPLIES, The Brooklyn Daily Eagle, 11/3/1889, p1

43. KURTH'S ADMISSION, The Brooklyn Citizen, 2/5/1891, p5

44. MCKANE AND FERGUSON, The Times Union, 11/14/1887, p1

45. THERE IS A COLDNESS NOW, The Times Union, 11/10/1887, p1

46. NOTHING WILL BE DONE, The Brooklyn Daily Eagle, 11/16/1887, p4

47. UNTITLED, The Times Union, 12/24/1887, p8

48. UNTITLED, The Brooklyn Daily Eagle, 1/1/1888, p15

49. MCKANE NOT SORRY, The brooklyn Daily Eagle, 1/6/1888, p6

50. CONEY ISLAND, The American Experience, 1990

51. CAPTAIN HINMAN'S STORY, The Brooklyn Daily Eagle, 1/31,1894, p9

52. UNTITLED, The Brooklyn Citizen, 1/31/1894, p4

53. ON A WELL-BEATEN PATH, The Brooklyn Citizen, 12/5/1893, p1

54. MCKANE IS NOW IN SING SING, The Brooklyn Daily Eagle, 3/1/1894, p1

55. APPOINTMENTS AT GRAVESEND, The Brooklyn Daily Eagle, 4/14/1894, p12

56. EUSTIS SUCCEEDS MCKANE, The Brooklyn Daily Eagle, 4/13/1894, p1

57. WHISTLING FOR THIE MONEY, The Brooklyn Daily

Eagle, 5/2/1894, p4

58. IS AN INSPECTOR, The Standard Union, 5/4/1894, p1

59. NO DIVES AND FAKE SHOWS, The Brooklyn Daily Eagle, 5/5/1894, p1

60. UNTITLED, The Standard Union, 5/7/1894, p5

61. GRAVESEND POLICE CANDIDATES, The Brooklyn Daily Eagle, 11/8/1895, p7

62. ONE FARE TO BEACHES, JUSTICE GAYNOR RULES, The Standard Union, 8/12/1906, p1

63. BRT CAN'T KEEP PUBLIC LOCKED UP IN BULL PEN, The Brooklyn Citizen, 8/14/1906, p12

64. UNTITLED, The Times Union, 8/13/1906, p1

65. COLER CALLS UPON SHERIFF TO CURB CITY POLICE, The Brooklyn Citizen, 8/14/1906, p12

66. REMOVAL OF BRT POLICE FOLLOWED BY DISORDER, The Brooklyn Citizen, 8/28, 1906, p4

67. HAD TO DISBAND FORCE, The Brooklyn Daily Eagle, 9/7/1906, p3

68. THE EXPERIMENT AT SEA GATE, The New York Times, 10/7/1906, p40